Phantom Son:

A Mother's Story of Surrender

Sharon Estill Taylor

Two Sylvias Press

Two Sylvias Press
PO Box 1524
Kingston, WA 98346
twosylviaspress@gmail.com

Cover Art: *Pink Imperial* by James B. Hartel
Interior Art: James B. Hartel
Cover Design: Kelli Russell Agodon
Book Design: Annette Spaulding-Convy
Author Photos: Dinea de Photo

Created with the belief that *great writing is good for the world*, Two Sylvias Press mixes modern technology, classic style, and literary intellect with an eco-friendly heart. We draw our inspiration from the poetic literary talent of Sylvia Plath and the editorial business sense of Sylvia Beach. We are an independent press dedicated to publishing the exceptional voices of writers.

For more information about Two Sylvias Press or to learn more about the eBook version of *Phantom Son* please visit: www.twosylviaspress.com

First Edition. Created in the United States of America.

ISBN: 13: 978-0692494653
ISBN: 10: 0692494650

Two Sylvias Press
www.twosylviaspress.com

Praise For *Phantom Son*

Dr. Sharon Estill Taylor has written a highly readable and illuminating account of her experience as a birthmother in the sixties. With a keen eye for detail and a wry sense of humor, she vividly recounts the ways the no-questions-asked cultural forces of the time swept her toward the surrender of her son. Though steamrolled by a process that gave her no say, Dr. Taylor persevered and found her voice as an early champion of sensitive search and reunion.

—**Jim Gritte**r, author of *The Spirit of Open Adoption, Lifegivers,* and *Hospitious Adoption*

&

In *Phantom Son*, Dr. Sharon Estill Taylor tells her own story of being an unwed mother at age 18 in the early 1960s. It bridges a time when unwed women endured devastating discrimination and pressure to give up their parental rights to a time when searching for and finding these children was more accepted and facilitated by society. There are smaller sub-stories, including one about the author's loss of her father who was killed in World War II, and how that event affected her family over the decades; and another about her experience of sex and identity-formation in the 1960s. These sub-stories are fascinating and contribute to the gripping nature of this book. Beyond all, this is a story of grief, courage, and redemption. The lives of most people are filled with issues and complexities that only can be addressed by storytelling. Taylor does that with grace and eloquence.

—**John Harvey**, Editor of the *Journal of Loss and Trauma*, and Professor of Psychology, Emeritus, University of Iowa

&

Dr. Sharon Estill Taylor's account of her unintended pregnancy and her subsequent traumatic adoption process in the 1960s is

an important reminder of how far we have come as a society in terms of the acceptance of out of wedlock births. Instead of the rampant shaming and secrecy surrounding these pregnancies, these commonplace events are now tolerated and even celebrated. This is how it should be as the impact of societal and religious silencing and shame heaped upon these mothers in the 1960s was nothing short of traumatic abuse, as Dr. Taylor tells us in her book. This is an important read for anyone, but I particularly recommend this book for those whose lives have been affected by the disenfranchised grief of coerced adoption.
—**Deborah Stokes, PhD**, Director of The Better Brain Center, Washington, DC

ॐ

In *Phantom Son*, Dr. Sharon Estill Taylor shares her journey as an unwed mother in the 1960s and her courageous search for the son she had to give up. Her grief and loss give way to the formation of wonderful familial relationships. In the tradition of the Irish story teller, Dr. Taylor gives her readers a powerful gift that will resonate in their own lives.
—**Fr. Kilian J. Malvey, O.S.B.**, Professor of Theology, Saint Martin's University

ॐ

As a reunited adoptee, I never tire of reading about reunions. In Dr. Sharon Estill Taylor's *Phantom Son,* the reader experiences the author's journey from love-struck teenager to expectant mother to powerful advocate for other birthmothers. Dr. Taylor vividly describes how she was forced to physically separate from her son and how she kept the emotional connection alive in her soul. Dr. Taylor's writing is raw, open, and honest; important qualities when dealing with such emotional subject matter.
—**Christine Murphy**, author of *Taking Down the Wall*

Acknowledgements

The words for *Phantom Son* are strung together with truth, lived experience, injustice, redemption, ancient ritual, young dreams, great loss, disenfranchised grief, and soaring joy. I mention the following people who have loved me and who believed that this is a story I should tell:

Lee Campbell and Concerned United Birthparents, without whom we would still be called unwed mothers and our children would be illegitimate.

Jim Gritter, who dared to pioneer Open Adoption. Imagine that.

Paul Rocca, you were the first to know my secret and you bought the cow anyway.

Andrea, Justin, Laura, for being ok with an extra surprise older brother and letting me mother you despite my feet of clay.

Mary and Hal Ravely, who would approve.

Mark Ravely, there's no one with whom I'd rather share the status of adopted sibling.

Delaney, Alexis, Noah and Ev, my bonus prizes for finding my phantom son.

1Lt. Shannon Estill, who left me his tenacity and bravery.

Nana Lettie and Nana Nell, for showing me how to be smart and pretty.

Banka, thank you for so elegantly stepping into your son's place.

Donna and Paul, who gave me shelter and safe passage.

Mary Frances, for doing what I couldn't and doing it well.

To the girls:

Carolyn Lilly, who stayed with me when the rats deserted the ship.

Roxanne Rossilion, Dora the Explorer has nothing on you! You are a true sister and the smartest girl I know.

Dr. Deb Stokes, with whom I transited a doc program that included Roman mischief and great irreverence.

Cay McClymont, my most perfect queen who always listens with love and wisdom.

Neecy, who helps me unpack my red luggage—what would I do without you?

Mozer, my first best friend.

Deb Gurley, for being in that brochure just when I needed to know you.

'Debby' Debow, for your great wisdom and for your resilience and grace under fire.

Mary Smith, my personal Nancy Drew.

Margaret Ann, for being my WingGirl at our 50th reunion.

I would also like to thank:

Jim Hartel, for your art, your dance moves, for introducing me to nine fine Irishmen, and for everything in between BDalton and now.

Thomas Humphrey, you had me at WTF.

Chuckles Keenan, my wise-assed knight in shining armor.

Hon. Mary R. Schowengerdt, who kicked open the final door.

Doreen McDonald, my first reader and stellar TA, who makes this professor proud.

For every student who signed up for my Grief and Loss seminar over the years and were willing to share their grief in exchange for mine. Those were the hours of healing and story telling that inspired me to write this down. I remember each of you with love.

Fr. Kilian, my Irish confidant with whom I will always be ready to share a Jameson.

John Harvey, for giving my father story a place in your journal (twice).

John Parsley, for LOST Mag, which gave me a yen to publish.

Dr. Jeff Birkenstein, LNS, always.

And Two Sylvias Press: Annette, my incomparable editor, who said, *we want this book* and who walked with me word for word, feeling for feeling, and took everyone I introduced her to on these pages into her heart. There are more Eggs Benedict in our future. Kelli, for a perfect Imperial cover, and to both of you for birthing Two Sylvias Press.

And Joe, for our inadvertent, but amazing legacy.

In the 52 years since these events transpired, I have forgotten little of who, what, where, and how. This is a lived experience that remains indelible. At the end of the day, I have sought and received "redemption," not in the religious sense, but *redemptive freedom* from the misguided belief that only the woman (or the girl) is responsible for getting pregnant. Forgive me the indelicacy, but please know that my goal in this book and in life is to be truthful, even if it doesn't make me the most popular girl at school.

If I've changed or deliberately not written a few names, I decided it was the least I could do since these individuals aren't here to provide their blessing. They know who they are, wherever they reside these days. I did my best to honor everyone in this story, and I did it with love. If I've forgotten anyone, I'll remember you in the sequel.

Table of Contents

for Raymond, to whom I owe the truth

Part I

There is no greater agony
than bearing an untold story inside you.

—Maya Angelou

I

Red Luggage

Des Moines

1963

When I got home from school that day, there was a complete set of American Tourister luggage arranged on my bed. It was a gift from my mother who had high hopes for the places where that luggage and I would travel. There was college in the fall, Europe for my junior year abroad, the homes of new friends, on trains and jets for holidays, and visits with my grandmothers in Oklahoma and Iowa where *red* luggage would be noticed. Those suitcases represented my future—like American Tourister advertised—*a toughness that won't break open* and those suitcases represented my mother's willingness to let me go.

My mother and I had a poignant relationship in which she regarded me with a sadness I could never soothe or capture. Now, I know it to be the result of losing the husband she loved deeply and being left with a daughter who reminded her of him every day. She was always my fierce and funny *little* mommy, smaller than me for more years than taller. War-widowed at twenty-three with a three-week-old daughter to consider, then remarried at twenty-seven, she had buried one husband, her father, and three babies by the time she was thirty-one. I was all that remained of her life with my father, a P38 fighter pilot in Germany, and the last man killed in his squadron just as World War II ended. Her grief was perpetual and unspoken. Despite her losses, she maintained a rare determination and a strong intelligence, occasionally interspersed with Irish joyful-sorrow. Her quick humor, rarely tempered and never lost in translation, frosted the layers of her life. Sometimes she looked at me as though my existence was a secret conduit to another level of being—the place, no doubt, where my father landed when he crashed. She was wistful for the romance she missed in his absence and I understood this as she struggled to close the space left by his absence. Even after she remarried, she maintained her secret vigil, and it wasn't out of the ordinary for her to whisper as she vacuumed or washed dishes, in a sweet, one-way conversation with herself.

What I remember about that *red luggage* day was that I had a secret, too. After my boyfriend, Joe, and I had sex for the first time a few months before, I had come right home, taken a bath, and jumped up and down in the bathroom so that if any sperm were making their way to the mother lode, I would be interrupting the passage. We knew these things to be true in 1963. If I'd consulted my mother with this flawed logic, I would have been embarrassed, but she would have set me straight, not only about jumping up and down to prevent pregnancy, but she would have intervened in what she perceived as my certain ruination. She was right on both counts. The birth control pill was still a clinical experiment on lab rats and on European women—Margaret Sanger's fortuitous and inspired dream. My options would have been to ask my mother for a diaphragm, which would have tipped her off to my snooping in her bureau and to my sexual activity. We had condoms, which were referred to as *rubbers*, and the brand Joe occasionally pulled out of his pocket was Trojan. Mostly, the two of us were impatient and impervious to the risks we were taking. While we feared pregnancy, we enjoyed having sex, and passion trumped worry. My parents were willing to talk about how children were created, but they didn't speak about how to prevent their conception. They were Catholic and the Church then, as now, didn't permit women to use any form of contraceptive. *What was the church thinking?* I would ask my mother this as she buried baby after baby, and would immediately become pregnant again. Many cards were stacked against a sexually active girl in the 1960s—I was supposed to be a virgin on my honeymoon.

My senior year of high school would end in June 1963, launching me on a direct trajectory to the University of Wisconsin. If things went according to my ideal plan, I would live with my valedictorian roommate, major in Journalism, meet college guys, leave Joe behind, and maybe meet the *man of my dreams*. I was certain that college life would be exactly as promised in the UW Campus Life brochure and maybe even better.

My mother was similarly charmed by my future. I was fulfilling her lost dreams and realizing her ambition, all in exchange for the necessary accouterments for my swift passage from a cloistered all-girls high school to a very public university. We dreamed it together.

Mom's latest contribution to the metamorphosis of daughter-to-coed, as college girls were euphemistically described, included this set of red luggage artfully arranged, just like a store display, on my twin bed. Included was my favorite, but least expected piece—the one deemed frivolous and *for later maybe*—the round hatbox. It had an impractical, single leather strap suitable for slinging over the arm and swaying in a jaunty fashion while navigating a train platform. *Look Magazine* ran a splashy ad with actress, Eva Marie Saint, surrounded by the entire seven-piece collection of red American Tourister luggage. She was supposedly checking into a Sheraton Hotel, while enjoying the attention of a doorman and a porter lugging two more red suitcases. This ad was pinned to the bulletin board above the desk in my bedroom.

My mother always pretended to be more practical than she was. She often said *no* first, *then* she considered what flawless logic would get the whole outrageous idea by my father—telling him *it was included free* or *it cost less than the actual price*. When she was desperate, she would say: *Nana sent it from Oklahoma*. My mother was a practiced secret-keeper, which would come in handy during the months to come.

Arranged with the rest of the luggage, this round red hatbox with carrying handle and ivory quilted lining exuded adulthood and glamour. It smelled like how I imagined *expensive* would smell, and it granted me the level of sophistication and A-line perfection I would need in college.

The train case was my favorite runner-up because in movie reality, the train case and the hatbox magically contained an entire wardrobe and hat collection. A removable white-marbled, plastic tray divided the train case into precious squares and oblongs, suitable to hold cosmetics and perfumes I didn't yet own or use. My cosmetic collection consisted of a few ill-conceived, unflattering, Woolworth lipsticks and a half-dozen bottles of Revlon nail polish with the tall, plastic plume, which adorned the top of each bottle. The only way for the nail polish to fit in the appropriate compartments was to lay them sideways, so inevitably, frosted pink oozed out and stuck forever to the plastic tray, identifying the case as belonging to a girl rather than a movie star.

The lining of the train case was of the same brocade, ivory quilt that matched the others. Years later, when I saw the casket of my friend's dead grandfather, I recognized the casket lining as eerily similar to that of my beloved red luggage. There was a mirror in the top lid of the train case inside an envelope that snapped. The mirror was more of an eventual liability than an asset because if the case were dropped, and the chances of that were certain, the mirror shattered into black-backed pieces, revealing an unbecoming industrial glue that blotted the elegant lining. I worried about these things.

The largest of the lot, the two-suiter, lent serious doubt to my ability to ever gracefully transport it without help. In the movies, a smiling porter would appear ready to follow a beautiful, disembarking train passenger who carried only her hatbox, while he transported the rest of her luggage on a massive, wheeled trolley.

The second smallest, *big* piece was a ladies dress and/or gentleman's suit bag. Rarely used, it became the middle child of the group, like my crabby sister Chris.

Taken as a set, without regard to individual limitations and idiosyncrasies, each case was resplendent in its own way. The linings were flawless, the little locks, the red, white, and blue luggage tags, and keys shaped like the face of a smiling bellhop, were included. I believed that American Tourister had created these special keys and locks exclusively for me.

Like a vintage movie moment on a train platform, I imagined unlocking the luggage to retrieve a monogrammed handkerchief or to tuck away the tiny, blue Tiffany box handed to me at the last minute by my doting older boyfriend who resembled Troy Donahue.

A stunning feature and one that glimmered with promise, charm, and Mrs. Jackie Kennedy style, was a sheet of oblong black and gold initials that could be selected, removed, and placed just under the handle of each bag. My chosen initials lent new cache to the set. *Let me just check the monogram and be certain these chic pieces of luggage are mine.* Romance attached itself to almost everything in my view.

During the preliminary luggage reconnaissance in the downtown Younker Brothers Department Store, where I also worked on Saturdays, my mother and I had serious discussions about the color choices available to the American Tourister customer. In the end, she chose the color I should have, and it was not as practical as she predicted. Besides red and black, there was another color choice, *fawn*, which I thought sounded elegant, but not half as dangerous as red. American Tourister fawn was the color of a good camel-hair coat with double buttons—the expensive kind with the little hairs that you could see only in the sun.

Fawn was *practical*, as my mother pointed out, and would easily match all of the flattering outfits that complimented my red hair. But I was drawn to the red leather of the suitcases and, if I were living her unlived dream, so was she. The train case, the hatbox, the biggest one, and the smaller big one were all on display. Each had an assigned function and each added immeasurably to my allure as a future college co-ed.

Mostly, I favored red rather than fawn because of my redheadedness. Redheads are a true minority, accounting for only 3% of the population with 100% of mothers who never allowed them to wear red. Fawn, on the other hand, was one of *my* colors. Red was not. Therefore, I was always drawn to red, and secretly I thought of it as naughty. Well, not naughty as much as statement-making-break-the-rules-sassy in that insouciant way *Seventeen Magazine* regarded as semi-sophisticated and risky. Red luggage exuded sassiness, and I coveted its inherent impracticality.

The entire set was expensive, and since my father was easily misled about prices, despite a career in retail management, the cost of this luggage was no exception. My mother warned me that telling my father the truth about certain things might cause him to have a heart attack. Husbands, in 1963, were not privy to how creatively their wives managed the household budget or their husbands' health.

My mother, pleased with the success of her surprise, went back to washing the bathroom floor. She left me to admire my luggage and play with the locks, keys, and initials. I sat on my bed and touched each piece, as if they were talismans that would erase my terror. I fervently wished to put everything back to where it was when I first noticed red luggage, when I was still a hopeful virgin.

I carefully arranged each piece as if in a magazine ad knowing the display would annoy my little sister, Chris, with whom I shared the bedroom. I went into the bathroom to reveal *my* surprise.

Mom was on her hands and knees on the floor, a cigarette burning in the ashtray on the edge of the bathtub, soapy water bucket nearby, in the familiar posture of *women's work* in those days. She let me tiptoe barefoot across the wet floor to sit on the closed toilet seat. I gazed longingly at her cigarette—I secretly smoked when I babysat for my brother and when I went out with Joe. Smoking was cool in the 1960s, accepted, and rarely discouraged even for teenagers. It was just another habit I kept to myself.

Mom looked so innocent and pleased with the

success of her luggage caper, however she paid for it. I hated to spoil her mood, but I asked, "If a girl misses her period, does it mean she's pregnant?"

My mother leaned back, sponge in hand, looking at me. Her glasses had slipped down her nose. She didn't attempt to adjust them, which gave her the faintly disapproving, professorial look I knew well.

"No, not necessarily, unless the girl has had sexual intercourse. If she hasn't had sexual intercourse," she rushed to add, "it's probably irregularity. Girls get busy with graduation, the prom, and thinking about college . . ."

If stress had been invented as a condition, she would have summoned it for the occasion.

"Did you have sexual intercourse, honey?" she asked.

"No! Jeez, Mom. I'm not like that."

"I'll just make an appointment with the doctor so you can quit worrying."

When, I wondered, *had I said I was worried?*

"Well," I snapped in my best prissy imitation of the virgin she believed me to be," I haven't done *that* so I couldn't be pregnant."

She immediately left the bathroom to call the doctor's office, half-clean floor abandoned. *Pregnant* was something my parents did, not me. I couldn't admit to being pregnant because it was 1963, and girls like me didn't do *that thing.* Also, pregnancy didn't happen to nice girls, only to wild girls who sinned, were of questionable intelligence, and had much larger breasts.

Her distant phone conversation with the doctor's office, muffled by the phone nook in the hallway, left me with her smoldering cigarette, and only the smallest nudge of pure panic wrapped nicely in denial.

Just a few minutes ago, the exact center of my world fit inside a perfectly matched set of red luggage, but now everything felt dangerously out of control. Lurking in my mind were the tentacles of the secret. My boyfriend and I had visited a doctor who would *take care of it.* I didn't realize until much later that this supposed *doctor* was sizing me up for an illegal abortion. He suggested, as a first attempt to change the course of my fate, that I drink some viscous substance he gave me in a glass of grape Hi-C. I only succeeded in gagging and acquiring a permanent aversion to Hi-C.

Our family doctor, who saw me within an hour of talking to my mother on the phone, asked me point blank if I had sex. I weighed my options, knowing I had to tell him the truth, unless I wanted to explain why Mary, the mother of Jesus, and I were the only two women to have found ourselves miraculously with child. Lying to a doctor was tantamount to lying to a priest.

After the examination, which mortified me in deepening degrees of despair, I sat with my mother and the doctor in his office. They were both smoking. It had started to rain and it was very dark for a June afternoon.

The doctor consulted a round, cardboard object with a twirly circle attached to dates in monthly increments, and pronounced me nearly two months pregnant and *due* in February. How could I be in this situation until February? I had planned to be away at the University of Wisconsin with my red luggage.

My mother must have had similar thoughts about the choices she would make on my behalf, but her gaze was impenetrable beneath layers of unfiltered Camel smoke. Perhaps she was thinking of an actual baby who would be her grandchild, or maybe she contemplated how she would be required to sublimate yet another loss because she was stoic by design. My mother may have worried about her church and all of the implications for a Catholic woman in 1963 to have a daughter *who got in trouble*. Was she pondering the concept of sin? Did her sister Madge, the nurse, cross her mind? Aunt Madge knew how to *fix* things, and she wasn't burdened with Catholic guilt. This situation was dire for my mother, and she had much to consider.

The saga of my pregnancy, which started that afternoon, involved topics like, *going away* and *living with a doctor's family in another state* and *is there a relative with whom she could stay for a few months?* and something referred to as *social services*. The red luggage surprise, the conversation in the bathroom with my mother, and the subsequent doctor's appointment all occurred on a Friday. My dad worked late on Friday nights and he always brought home a large meaty pizza after a quick stop at the Savery Hotel Bar. I was usually out with my boyfriend on Fridays, but tonight would be the first Friday of many that I would be home for the pizza.

My impression of this day was not just a blur; it evaporated from my consciousness. I sat on the back-screened porch in the rain and waited for the nightmare to jolt me awake. The phone began to ring with invitations for my usual Friday night out with friends, but my mother didn't come out on the porch to get me. I did sneak to the phone at some point to call Joe, and I was disappointed that he didn't answer. Dreading my father's arrival and having to talk to him about my day, I waited by myself.

Fear of my father's reaction to what my mother

must have already told him with a phone call after we had returned from the doctor, was based on an idle threat that he occasionally spoke: *making me rock my mistake if I ever got pregnant before I was married.* Instead, when he got home that night, he gathered me into his capable arms and promised *we'd* get through this together.

His words were the cue that I had one last chance to exonerate myself and be returned to my former image as a *good daughter.* It was clear that my parents would solve this problem, and I would comply. I was bargaining hard and fast with myself, begging my father's forgiveness for something about which I wasn't really sorry. And, there was the embarrassment factor, so I apologized for that, too. Getting caught having sex was one thing for a teenage girl, but becoming *pregnant* after having sex was a mortal sin. I worried about being banished to a strange place where there were even more unknowns, and I wondered why Joe would be able to live his life without any change. The topic of Joe was off limits at this moment, so I didn't mention him. If I had, I'm sure my father would have an opinion that was colored with male bravado.

In the end, my parents would come up with an imperfect plan, and I would agree to everything they decided to do. Because I wasn't directly asked about my feelings and ideas, I put my faith in my parents, believing that they knew what was best for me and for the baby. The baby? Wait a minute; I had stuff to do.

In 1963, the line between genders was clearly defined. Girls were put into either good or bad designations, which could shift easily and without warning. Boys were just boys. Being a *good* girl meant that you either appeared to be virginal and obedient to all of the moral and ethical regulations or that you were, in reality, virginal and rule compliant. No extra points were received either way. This good and bad compartmentalizing was the norm, and you were judged accordingly. *Bad* meant that you were a girl who was definitely suspect in the virginal role because you flaunted your disregard for the moral rules, and you were subsequently punished by an unfair god by getting *caught* without the safety net of marriage.

If even a whisper or rumor of sexual impropriety attached itself to a girl, she could slip from the *good* to the *bad* column by sunrise. My fall was sudden, but incremental. It was precipitated by a lethal combination of sloe gin mixed with 7UP, and slower dancing with a blonde boy who courted seduction. I was so far into the *good* girl column, I figured that I was always blessed with wisdom and protection from at least one dead relative, and my Catholicism had impressed upon me the consequences of giving in to temptation. Saints who were also in their teenage years had died for far less infractions of the moral code.

I hadn't considered sex as something I would or would not do, though I tended toward *would not do,* if asked. It seemed easier, considering I had little sexual experience, except for sweaty kissing with one or two boys I knew from school, and to whom I was prepared to say, *I am waiting for marriage.* They ended up never asking. Sex, as in naked, entangled, body parts, penises, and everything else, seemed an unattractive, inelegant, and embarrassing option. I never looked at myself in the mirror when I was naked, mostly because I was rarely naked and never near a mirror when I was. I just wasn't that curious about my body. I did experience a primal stirring when I read *Peyton Place,* watched Troy Donahue in *Parrish* or *Summer Place*, or listened endlessly to Tab Hunter sing, "Young Love": *They say for every boy and girl there's just one love in this whole world, and I, I, I, I've found mine.* To actually *do it* was beyond me in more than one hundred ways.

When *it* finally happened, I considered the event an out of body experience. It was Joe's seventeenth birthday. We never talked about having sex before we did it, except for me saying *no* with declining conviction. As we were doing *it* for the first time, he told me what a good birthday present I was giving to him and that he *loved me, baby.* Once that bridge was crossed, I realized it was a gift I could keep on giving and receiving—I wanted to be with him forever. I would have put money on the fact that he felt the same way about me. Joe and I simply incorporated my new willingness to have sex into most of our dates. There was a catchy little phrase about being unable to stop once you've started, and it certainly qualified as a bell impossible to unring.

With fresh sin marring my soul, Joe became my new religion. I adored him, and like all teenage girls who fall in love, I adored the way I felt when I was with him. I embraced my sexuality and I had my senior picture retaken so I could wear a slightly tighter black sweater rather than the light-blue, Cashmere, collared one my Iowa Nana had sent me from Saks Fifth Avenue in New York. I thought black a far more appropriate depiction of my secret, non-virginal status.

As a pregnant unwed teenager in 1963, the choices I had were to give the baby up for adoption or give the baby up for adoption. That was it. Though Joe and I made plans that involved me finding a job and him finishing high school, his parents quickly separated us from that fanciful idea. When I asked him what he thought we should do next, he sweetly answered that he would have to get a new sport coat for the wedding.

One evening, I eavesdropped on the only meeting between his parents and my parents. I heard his mother announce, *I'll get fifteen boys to say they've had sex with your daughter.* At the time, I knew it was insulting, but beyond that, it was the timeless roar of a mother lion protecting her boy cub. My father roared back defending me. Joe's parents left in haste and never spoke to my mom and dad again. We were on our own.

Decades later, I learned that my mother had called an old boyfriend of mine, one of the only boys I had kissed besides Joe, and she asked him if he would marry me. It's a nice story, but only sweet speculation that my mother, who suffered no fools, especially male fools, would go begging on my behalf.

I was now forbidden to see or talk to Joe. I'd already watched him drive by my house with a new girl in his car as he left from work at the country club, which was just up the street. It seemed ironic that my parents were rushing to close the barn door now. The particulars of my pregnancy dilemma became public knowledge when our family doctor told his wife and daughter about my visit to his office that June afternoon. I presume he warned his daughter to stay away from me, which she did, along with every girl to whom she told my supposed secret. I was an instant outcast among my peers, though a few of the boys I knew from school suddenly found me interesting. I flunked geometry because of the stress and had to retake it in summer school before I could officially graduate. Bad became worse; I was pregnant and puking in Dante's circles of hell.

I still went to my high school prom with Mike, a kind guy who wasn't a boyfriend, but was usually my date for our Catholic school dances. At St. Joseph Academy for Girls, we weren't allowed to attend dances with our non-Catholic boyfriends, and this was enforced under the watchful eye of the nuns and one old priest. I felt lucky and thankful to be allowed to attend the prom at all, much less have a date. For one night, I could pretend myself un-pregnant and living my alternate life in which I would go away to college in the fall.

Mike brought me an orchid corsage instead of the traditional gardenia, which further bolstered my *pretend* mood. A white orchid corsage, already in its death throes toward brown, signified a special occasion, and it was a significant investment for a kid with a paper route.

Because I had no interest in shopping for prom dresses, I had borrowed a dress from a friend. It was an emerald-green satin column with a train more appropriate for a bridesmaid in a December wedding than a high school prom in a humid June in Iowa. While the dress was lovely and long, it was also heavy. The unfortunate train concealed the half-open zipper down my back. My body had begun its gradual ascent from my less-than-100-pound frame, and I was getting thicker in all the places that would give away my secret. This train hid my sins so that I (and the dress) easily passed the nuns' pre-prom modesty inspection. Mike and I aced the test as we entered the Val Air Ballroom in West Des Moines.

I graduated a few weeks later with both of my grandmothers (who didn't suspect anything about my condition), my paternal grandfather, two aunts, and my parents in attendance. Later that night, I went out with some of my new friends who were much wilder than I had ever been. We were stopped by the cops for having four six-packs of Grain Belt beer in the trunk of the car. I was singled out and brought home by one of the officers who knew my dad from the Rotary Club. After this incident, I never saw those friends again. My sense was that I belonged nowhere. My invisibility had begun.

One night right after graduation, I was visited by a friend from the Catholic boy's high school, who worked as a part-time disc jockey at the radio station. His work made a short, humorous guy with a good voice popular, and we had become casual friends, though we never dated. Charley was an outrageous flirt, on and off the air, and he often stopped by my house in the radio station car along with the radio station German Shepherd, to bring me record albums and other prizes that the station gave away to listeners. I had an open invitation to "visit him" some evening at the station.

It became clear that Joe hadn't experienced a lull in his dating life since my parent-imposed sequester, and I wanted him think that I wasn't waiting for him. Obviously, my pregnant condition wasn't the city's best-kept secret, and I didn't have a prayer of finding a replacement boyfriend to flaunt in his face. The fishbowl radio studio was along the loop that my friends and I cruised up and down on weekends—our ultimate goal was to see and be seen, so passing by the "fishbowl" and waving to the disc jockeys was part of our ritual.

One Friday night, I took Charley up on his offer to visit the studio, and a friend dropped me off about an hour before my curfew. I thought it would be interesting to see what might happen in a fishbowl with a disc jockey. Charley and I sat together as he played music—The Beach Boys, The Shirelles, The Dave Clark Five, The Kingston Trio, The Lettermen, Jan and Dean, Leslie Gore, Roy Orbison, Elvis Presley, Bobby Vinton, Paul Anka and The Beatles, who had just become popular in the UK. He waved to people passing by and chatted with those who stopped at the studio window to watch what might have been considered *celebrity behavior* in 1963.

This was the visibility I wanted, and I behaved in unexpected and paradoxical ways. I wanted Joe to hear about my evening in the fishbowl, and I wanted him to believe that he had been replaced, despite my *situation.* I had so few defenses against the pain of Joe's abandonment that this radio station stunt was the best revenge I could come up with. Perhaps Charley had invited me there after hearing the rumors about my loose moral character, and maybe he felt that he had gotten lucky as we ended up having a quick and inept sexual encounter in the control room of the radio station. At best, the sex was rushed, and at worst, I was mortified at my impulsive behavior. I worried for the next seven months, wondering if it were possible to get pregnant while already being pregnant. Mostly, I hoped Joe would find out that I wasn't waiting for him. Of course, in reality, I *was* waiting for him, and I wanted to die, but not actually be dead forever.

My friend's car arrived at the studio to take me home, and it was so crowded that I had to squeeze into the back seat with three other girls. What were the odds that the girl I sat next to and pressed to the door, would be Joe's current girlfriend? I had seen them together a few times, and I figured out that they were dating. She gave me the evil eye, and I knew that Joe had told her my secret. We didn't speak to each other in the car, although I could clearly feel her imperious assessment of me and my situation. This new girlfriend of Joe's seemed the perfect conduit, since I wanted him to know about my late night visit with Charley at the radio station.

I never saw the disc jockey again, and at a high school reunion decades later, I was told he had recently died. Some things are better left unexplored, but from my experience in the radio station, I did learn that I wasn't a fan of casual or retaliatory sex. Dorothy Parker suggests that "revenge is best served cold." There was nothing constructive about my plan to appear normal by acting in an abnormal way. Joe never looked back, and I had nowhere to go but forward. There was no revenge to be served cold or otherwise by a powerless and invisible teenage girl.

With school over and summer school looming, I waited in the wings of my parents' theatre of the absurd, for the next act. My social life, as I knew it, was over. My body was changing and betraying me with nausea and exhaustion. Mostly, I slept and waited. As adoption options were explored, I barely heard the daily reports my mother transmitted from the brave new world she was investigating. She was good at surviving by keeping busy—doing anything and calling it "making Limóncello from lemons" and creating a disappeared daughter from a pregnant one.

When my mother tried to act pleased, after

learning I had been invited to live with a doctor and his family in Kansas, for the first time I wondered why I couldn't simply have this baby and keep it. There was a charming, old apartment building on Grand Avenue near my high school, which reminded me of the area in Iowa where Nana lived. I could move into the apartment with the baby, go to college, and work at the Younkers department store. I thought this was a plan worth examining. My father responded to me with his resoundingly flawed logic, offered from a residing and timeless sexist belief that declared, *no man will ever have you again if you have a kid and you are not married*. Even then, it didn't ring true to me, but he seemed so sure, and who was I, after all, to argue with my own redemption?

The main option my parents and I considered involved me leaving Iowa to live with a benevolent doctor's family, where I would be required to fulfill all expectations of a humble, trite, obedient houseguest and babysitter. Who knew there were doctors housing unmarried, teenage pregnant girls? Were they safe or punitive? No one asked me for my opinion, but I would have preferred napping for the next seven months.

We tried an ill-conceived visit to social services, "just to explore other options," my mother said, and it ended up horrifying her. The social worker never looked at us, but stared at a file on her desk. Her office was so small and so dark, I wondered how she could read whatever was written on the papers.

"Is the father of this baby a Negro?" she asked my mother.

"Why is that important?" my mother replied with an edge that spoke more to indignation than information.

"If this were a half-Negro child, it would be

unadoptable, that's why."

I could see my mother's Irish emerging as she gathered her purse to leave. This was her lost grandchild, and "unadoptable" wasn't possible. My mother made it clear that we would handle my pregnancy and subsequent adoption our own way and that her daughter would not participate in a social service system that judged a baby's value in this manner.

As a result of that misguided social work visit, my parents discarded all possible options, except for me hiding out in the doctor's house in Kansas. I was expected to feel privileged and grateful for the opportunity. I struggled to feel any gratitude, but was reminded by my parents that other unwed pregnant girls, considered *two and three time offenders*, were doomed to distant maternity homes, many of which were in Kansas City. I was told that such a home, with those inherently promiscuous women in residence, was unacceptable for me to live in. There was a fear that I might be unduly influenced to repeat my mistake—as if witnessing other girls suffering in my situation would glorify this slut-shaming we were sharing, as if the genie could be stuffed back into her sex chamber and all feelings forgotten.

The red luggage no longer represented hope or an enthusiastic transition to the future. If anything, it stood in the place of my former happiness. The suitcases were eventually moved to the basement, where my father covered them with a paint cloth as though they were cadavers. When I left for Kansas to live with the doctor's family, I took a small, older suitcase and would borrow or buy the few items I would need there. I was a traveler and no stranger to packing for adventures. Instead of filling every one of those red suitcases, I packed as if I were going to prison, where everything would be provided and nothing would be familiar. Along with my baby, I would leave behind the suitcase and everything else, when I returned home in February.

My mother and I flew to Kansas City in August, and what I most remember was my surrender to sorrow. I had finally faced and distanced myself from the reality I was living. My mother clung fervently to the armrest of the plane praying, she told me later, that she was doing the right thing and that I would be acceptable to the doctor, his wife, and to the parents who would adopt my baby. My new secret, which I didn't tell my mother, was that when this pregnancy was over, I intended to have Joe back in my life.

II
Blue Gant Shirt
Des Moines
1962

A heavy wool sweater, emblazoned with a letter *D; a* cumbersome, nearly ankle-length, pleated, corduroy skirt; and official, Wigwam wool socks in red saddle shoes—this comprised the girls and the boys (with pants not skirts) cheerleading uniforms of St. Joseph Academy. The outfit contributed more to extreme modesty than to jumping around in front of strangers. Of course, that was the point.

I was grateful for serious hairspray, which granted my anxious, independent Irish hair no freedom. Along with the other cheerleaders, in varying stages of teen girl hysteria, we joined the halftime crowd outside the gym of the Dowling Catholic Boys School. It was a particularly frigid January evening for a basketball game in Iowa, but we were sweating in our wool and corduroy uniforms. I was surprised when a boy from the opposing school came up to me and started talking about the friends we had in common. To say he was *social* would be an understatement—he still had friends from preschool. I thought, *this guy is cuter than Tab Hunter and Troy Donahue combined.* He was a popular, public school boy who swam and played baseball when he wasn't working as a lifeguard at a country club. And here he was inviting *me* to come to a party after the game, and he mentioned that it would be at an *older guy's* house, which translated to: *There will be liquor and no parents.* While he sauntered away with an over-the-shoulder smile that I found irresistible, I told my best friend, Carolyn, that we were going to a party after the game. Carolyn had a car, which provided our unsupervised independence, and she agreed with the intriguing offer I had just received.

We navigated the winter roads with the radio blasting our favorite DJ, Dick Biondi, all the way from WLS in Chicago, and we speculated about what was surely going to be a forbidden and fabulous party. My parents were confidently overprotective of me as their eldest child, and my experience with boys was glaringly innocent compared to what we encountered in that basement. Booze was indeed being served, but not in the tradition of my father's complex preference for dark Manhattans—a bracing mixture of bourbon and sweet vermouth, fat maraschino cherries, and a dash of bitter truth. And not the cut crystal goblets of sweet Port, which my mostly non-drinking mother sipped as she cooked dinner and prepared for my father's reentry. I accepted a sloe gin and 7UP, which gave me an embarrassing case of the hiccups.

This was the first time I saw Joe, sitting on the arm of a couch and talking to a girl who seemed enraptured by him. When he noticed me and crossed the room—all blue eyes, blue shirt, khaki trousers, Weejun penny loafers, blond surfer hair, and a killer smile, I melted. We talked about the game, his friends, our favorite music, and the movies we wanted to see. Standing around, beers and sickeningly sweet drinks in hand, we mimicked the behavior of our parents at a cocktail party.

We danced in that overcrowded space filled with people who were strangers to me. I liked them because they were so much more sophisticated than the kids I usually hung out with, and they were *his* friends. As we danced, I touched his shoulder beneath the crisp, blue shirt, and I realized that I felt an overwhelming attraction. He was not impervious to the way he looked in blue, pinpoint cotton, which exactly matched his eyes, nor was I.

This basement crowd of Joe's friends was a marked departure from the awkward Catholic boys from

Dowling for whom I had sweated and led cheers earlier that night. It was obvious to me that the boys at this party were Protestants, definitely less silly than the unsophisticated Catholic boys, and obviously more worldly. I felt worldly myself in this group, drinking my pink cocktail, and chatting with this blue-eyed boy who danced like one of the men in *Peyton Place*. I was still overheated from the inside-outside winter air, but not only because of that—I had developed a train wreck of a crush on this guy, and I knew it was time to go home.

I was expected to leave with Carolyn because, according to my parents' rules, I had to come home by midnight with whoever had given me a ride. If not, I had to call my father to pick me up. This applied to all dates with boys and going out with girlfriends. Calling my father for a ride home from tonight's party would be a request he wouldn't appreciate. I imagined him coming to the door and asking to meet the parents who didn't live there. I could see him busting us for drinking then calling the police. My father once notified the authorities when the Catholic boys from Dowling strung toilet paper around all of the trees on our wooded property. I had assured my father that this was the boys' way of welcoming me into town, but he called them *destructive little Nazis*.

When Carolyn and I left the party, Joe walked us to the car and said to me, "I'll give you a call."

On the ride home, I barely noticed my friend's excited chatter as she spoke about all of the cute guys at the party; I knew I had crossed a major line—I had found the boy of my dreams and something unexpected and sexual was awakening in me. I had done it all in my dopey cheerleading outfit and the nuns at St. Joseph's would be disturbed on many levels.

I could hardly focus after the party, and I didn't breathe again until the phone finally rang a few days later.

"I hear you're good at journalism and writing," Joe said.

"Pretty good, why?"

My best subjects in high school were journalism and English, and I was instantly grateful that he wasn't asking for math advice.

"If I show you what I'm writing for my journalism class, will you tell me what's wrong with it?" *God,* I thought, *he needs me,* and I agreed to help him before he finished his sentence.

"Great. Why don't we go to a show tomorrow night and I'll bring my paper."

We planned to drive some distance to one of the big downtown theatres. When Joe met my parents, my father later declared, "The kid has a good handshake."

My mother was non-committal, but flushed slightly at his attention and offered some cautionary tale about going downtown at night. Though I had no sexual experience, I'd had a semi-serious relationship that involved declaring love and making out with a boy in his father's Pontiac Star Chief. On most weekends, I babysat, visited my girlfriends, or ended up grounded for some shadowy infraction, such as, *being mouthy or having a bad attitude.* I believe now that the groundings were a ruse so that my parents had a babysitter. I was not (yet) rebellious, but I was opinionated and demanding. I always seemed to be in trouble—my parents were practicing everything they would never do later with subsequent siblings. The oldest child is always the grand experiment in parenting. My mother told me with no apology that she and my father had learned from their mistakes with me, and therefore they would do things differently with my brothers and sister.

Joe and I crossed the icy sidewalk to his 1956 Dodge Royal Lancer convertible, which was his mother's car and shared with his sisters, but would be the future scene of many transgressions and high drama. The temperature was significantly below freezing, so I resisted throwing my coat in the backseat and sliding across the wide bench seat to sit next to him. As I realized the charm of something yet unnamed but definitely seductive, I found myself rushing toward the pinnacle of romance, which I barely understood. With what was left of my propriety, I stayed near the passenger door, never removing my mittens nor unfastening my top coat button. My instincts were honed for caution, but I flipped the switch to foolhardy before the car heater kicked in, and there my sensibility remained.

My destiny was unfurling in front of me, and with Joe, I felt taller, cuter, more elegant, and *Yes, I'd love a cigarette. Old Gold filters, my favorite, too.* I lied sweetly. I preferred menthol cigarettes as they were easier to steal from my father, but here I was, already trying to please. Although I didn't smoke very much, it was on my list of *things to do well* one day. Everyone who was cool in 1962 smoked. He lit his cigarette, then mine. I hoped he didn't notice that I wasn't very adept at smoking, except to mimic my mother.

The fine details of this first date are mingled with many subsequent dates of that spring. The movie showing that month at the downtown Paramount Theatre was *Lawrence of Arabia.* Next door, was a little record store where customers could sit in a soundproof booth and listen to the latest 45 rpm records. My parents believed strongly that nothing good could happen after midnight and that nothing bad could happen before. *Getting home by midnight* meant being inside the house, not parked in front until 12:30. That night, we parked long enough for him to kiss me. By the time he walked me to the door, I had entered a state of breathlessness and bliss wherein I could feel our chemistry eroding my *convictions and my virtue,* whatever still remained of them.

In my teenage wisdom, the events of that first date were the genesis of a template for true love. I began to construct a model—*a fantasy*—for romance. This collection of feelings and impressions allowed me to elevate Joe to the status of *most important boy in the world, for whom I would do anything*. I had found *love. In love with love* was one of my mother's favorite witticisms, which she often said to me. What I didn't know yet, though I would learn, was that boys give love to get sex, while girls give sex to get love. At least this is what urban mythology told us then.

Joe and I spent a lot of time on the phone during the week when I wasn't allowed to go out at night. He'd read me the articles he was writing for his journalism class, which I found fascinating and brilliant. He was fun to talk to; he had a million ideas about life that I hadn't thought of, and at least as many friends, many of whom he'd known since nursery days.

We spent countless hours in his car, at the movies, and with his friends at motel parties, which were crowded with unsupervised, under-aged drinkers. Joe would pick me up after school nearly every day, and I would lie to my parents, telling them that I was getting a ride with Carolyn. I was allowed to ride with Carolyn, although she once crashed into a parked vehicle because we were flirting with a station wagon full of boys driving in the lane next to us. Later at our fiftieth high school reunion, Carolyn told me that her family never forgave her for wrecking the car in such an inelegant manner, and that she never lived it down.

After school, Joe waited for me at the end of the long walk from the sheltered portico entry to St. Joseph's, where the principal, Sister Mary Denis, watched our departure. Saint Joseph Academy for Girls, a former boarding school, had been built, we surmised, by St. Joseph the Carpenter. It was also the antithesis of the public high school where Joe enjoyed a more liberal, less traditional, education and freedom.

After he picked me up, we'd usually stop at Henry's Hamburgers, just down the hill from the school, for a burger and a Coke. After that, we would go someplace where we could dance and make out for a few hours before I was expected home for dinner. This became our routine, and somehow, I managed to create a shield of innocence that even my parents couldn't penetrate.

Joe's seventeenth birthday was on a Friday night in late March. My eighteenth birthday had been the week before. He was a year behind me in school, but I was certain he was years ahead of me in life. Neither talk show psychology nor examining logic existed in mainstream consciousness in 1963. It did not occur to me to question why I endowed Joe, a boy I'd only recently met, with such sophistication and power. I attributed his choice of me as his girlfriend to my Irish luck and to the blessing of my dead relatives.

I was a member of the Younker's Department Store Teen Board, the same store where my mother would buy the red luggage. My job, as one of two selected Teen Board representatives from my school, was to work on Saturdays selling clothes in the junior department to my friends. We also modeled outfits, shoes, hats, and coats in the tearoom. My mother and grandmother liked to attend these shows and watch my pseudo-sophisticated imitation of Susie Parker, my favorite New York runway model. I looked forward to lunch after the show, which was always a Rarebit burger with fancy shoestring fries, and a lemon Coke.

On the night of Joe's birthday, I had to work the next day and my grandmother, an actual model who earned a living wage from it, was coming to the tearoom for lunch. Since living in the moment was an art children and teenagers perfect, I was determined to make his birthday memorable.

The wavy vision, or what I'd like to believe about that night, fit into my romantic template nicely. Of course, Joe wore a blue Gant shirt, and he said the words I wanted to hear in the way he had of neutralizing my resistance. Our romance was heading off a cliff. Sexual tension, coupled with too many sloe gin fizzes, took us to the place we'd been heading for the past two months. Parents never account for, or they forget about, the sea change, which happens when teenage girls mix blue shirts and booze with the perfect opportunity.

What I remember about the act of losing my virginity is that it hurt for a minute, I made a noise, and Joe put his hand over my mouth. He said, "I love you, baby." We had left our group of friends and found a dark unfinished room in the basement that housed a furnace and a dank, questionably clean bed.

The record player was loud, the lights were off, and couples were necking all over the place. We had been at the party long enough to drink too much booze with too little caution—of course, we ended up in the back room of the basement.

I had been resisting having sex with him, not by talking about it, but by stopping the action when we would make out and fool around in his car. My fading resistance was paltry against the strong attraction I felt, coupled with a gallon of sloe gin and 7UP.

That night my virginity was dispensed with and replaced with the chemical reaction that women experience after sex. It would be decades before I learned that just as men's dopamine is released and they *detach*, women's oxytocin arrives, and they become *attached*. I had been ambivalent and focused on fending off any actual intercourse in favor of the fun of partially dressed foreplay, but now I began to feel that the only way to keep Joe was to have sex with him.

My sense of self didn't allow for discernment or saying *no* to him. He said, *I love you*, we had sex, and the connection was made. This was *love*. I didn't really experience pleasure that first time as much as haste. We did it nearly each time we saw each other thereafter, and I learned to enjoy it, but my main concern was keeping him happy so that he would never leave me.

In my adolescent logic and newfound sexual urgency, I came to believe that this was how the deepest feelings between boys and girls were expressed. I had to believe that Joe's love for me wasn't contingent upon my willingness to have sex, wherever, whenever, and often. Sex seemed to create in my brain a confection of forbidden pleasure and danger. I was making this choice for myself—my first independent decision about which I hadn't solicited my parents' sage advice, reluctant approval, or permission. Like most teenagers, I was afraid to speak to my mom and dad about sexuality, as I knew they would blame Joe and make us break up. I did not have a working knowledge of natural consequence, and birth control was an inconvenience. I had it all figured out, until I didn't.

To say that I wasn't emotionally ready for sex can only be determined in hindsight. Some lessons are better learned by experience, even if the consequence is disastrous. Although my original goal had been to wait for sex until marriage, as was expected by church and society, some part of my addled teenage brain had decided that Joe was the only man with whom I would ever have sex.

I really didn't think it would make a difference if I got pregnant, and like the decision to have sex the first time, Joe and I never discussed the possibility of conceiving a child. Joe didn't like condoms because they created the sensation of *wearing a raincoat in the shower,* which was the companion logic to why male orgasms were necessary because *it hurts too much not to*. By not having sex with Joe, I risked being labelled a *tease*. In 1963, sex just happened to women. Talking about it somehow spoiled the soap opera magic of whatever was implied at *fade to black*.

After having sex in that dank basement room, we drove home drunk and on time.

At work the next day, I wore the red wool dress that all the Teen Board girls wore that year. It was chosen by our fashion coordinator, Nadine Gunson, along with black kitten-heeled pumps, and a plastic name tag that identified us and our school. I had been chosen as the senior along with a pretty junior from Saint Joseph's, and it was more exciting than anything I'd accomplished in high school. I'd only been at Saint Joseph's for three semesters, and my last semester was filled with activities. I'd situated myself among the smug, popular rich girls though I was neither. I still remained loyal to my friend, Carolyn, who continued to drive us everywhere and with whom I enjoyed a genuine and deep friendship.

I drove infrequently because the car my father had purchased that year was a hideous, pink and black Dodge Comet with obnoxious fins. He said its ugliness was his assurance that I wouldn't want to drive it. I avoided that car because my position as *the new girl* remained tenuous.

I decided to accept Des Moines as my new home, though I still loved the small Wisconsin town we had left behind. My friends there were different, less frantic, less pressured, more ambitious, and inclusive. I was a big fish in a nice small pond. Having moved to my third high school half way through my junior year, I struggled for acceptance as a new girl, but having a cute boyfriend heightened my status and esteem. I was involved with as much social activity as my mediocre grades allowed. Being a cheerleader was no small accomplishment, since we tried out and were chosen by the students at the boys' school, a couple of Jesuit priests, and our nuns. I remember the day the meager squad of three girls and three boys was announced. I'd had a lackluster tryout, since my athleticism was limited to skiing and tennis—an athletic girl's body wasn't in fashion in the early 1960s—so it was shocking to hear our principal, Sister Mary Denis, call my name during the announcements.

The first cheer practice was held in my large backyard. My mother volunteered to knit matching, angora and wool crescent-shaped hats that protected our ears and tied under our chins with tiny burgundy pompoms on the ties. She also bought out the burgundy and white crepe paper from my father's Woolworth store and helped us make rustling pompoms for the games; our hands were stained burgundy for a week.

It had been a good semester. I had a boyfriend who *loved* me, and the right crowd finally accepted me, including the class valedictorian who wanted to be *my* roommate in college. I had a great job with a discount at the store where everyone shopped for Villager and Ladybug clothes. I had my hair done in the store salon almost every week. And, last night during Joe's birthday party, my life had changed for the better, or so I thought. Looking at myself in the three-way mirror in the junior department, I thought, like Alice in Wonderland, *Curious. I don't look different, but I should.*

My Iowa Nana watched the fashion show in the tearoom that Saturday and praised my efforts at sophistication, though I knew her flattery was the kind gesture of a good Nana. She spoke to the Teen Board Director about how to better train us as models: *Don't dress them like the women they aren't yet. And, never let them model fur coats or wedding dresses.*

My Nana commanded respect and attention for other things in addition to her gorgeous face and body, and she knew the fashion business. I wanted to be just like her when I grew up. When her husband died in 1939, leaving her with six children, she counted her assets and resources, then went to work as a model and a saleswoman in a posh department store.

Widows surrounded me, it seemed, including my mother, whose loss of her young husband, my biological father, had forever robbed her of joy. The thought of living without true love was unimaginable to me. I wanted to remain as happy as I was at that very moment, and I never wanted to be alone. I wondered if my Nana noticed the change in me, now that I was no longer a virgin. Nothing mattered more than seeing Joe that night, and it was my fervent wish to be asked to wear the wedding dress in the next fashion show.

During my fifteen-minute break, I took the escalator down to the men's department to touch the starchy, blue Gant shirts and inhale English Leather and Canoe, the colognes Joe always wore on our dates. I sprayed each cologne on the sample fragrance papers at the perfume counter, and then tucked them into my Playtex bra under my red Teen Board dress—like secret talismans of our "love." The sexual dice had been cast, and I had become a *woman* in the space of eighteen hours.

III

Pink Imperial

Kansas City

1963 - 1964

My mother smoked unfiltered Camels from Des Moines to Kansas City, taking full advantage of the metal ashtray built into the armrest of her airplane seat. I would have smoked, too, but the flight, and my trepidation about our destination, rendered me nauseous. It still wasn't a sin or a medical mistake to smoke during pregnancy in 1963—my mother had smoked the seven times she'd been pregnant.

The plane landed in the middle of the runway, and stairs were rolled up to the exit door. This September afternoon in Kansas City was almost balmy and it was a Sunday. My mother would spend the rest of the day getting me settled a*t the doctor's* house, where I would live for the next five months until I gave birth. The doctor's wife was meeting us at the airport, and the doctor would drive my mother back for her return flight that evening. She had instructed us, in her breezy letter, to collect my luggage, come to the main airport entrance, and to look for a pink Chrysler Imperial. I wondered if pink cars were to be my curse.

When we read about the Chrysler in her letter, despite the heaviness of my expulsion from Des Moines, my mother and I looked at each other and grinned. My ride to banishment would be in a pink car. From a beige Chevy and Ford family of functional cars (but for the brief interlude with the ugly pink and black model), this was a stunning step up. Outside the Kansas City airport, we spotted the Imperial in all its pink be-finned glory, waiting to take me where I could live the anonymous life of an unwed mother—a knocked-up bun-in-the–oven girl of questionable morals and dubious judgment. I was a spoiled one—a *slut* by current standards. Nonetheless, *this slut* was picked up at the airport in a pink Imperial.

Neither my mother nor I had ever heard of nor had we ever seen a pink Imperial, but I followed her lead and acted casual and unimpressed. We acted as if we'd ridden in hundreds of upscale Chryslers with many doctors' wives as we drove toward my exile. I doubted there were any other *pink* cars at the Kansas City airport on that day in history. I felt special, as though I had received a sign of hope and redemption from that gorgeous car, along with a nod of acceptance.

Yes, I thought, *this banishment at the doctor's home will be interesting.*

The doctor's wife was as big-boned and smiley as my mother was tiny and serious. She seemed happy and organized and very much in charge of us as she merged onto Ward Parkway toward home. She drove and talked fast, and she shared the ashtray on the sparkly dash with my mother. It was hidden behind a small silver door that when opened, presented the ashtray like an appetizer. What I noticed about my mother was that she had assumed her bridge-club face, and she seemed too small in the front seat. Later, she told me that she felt comforted in the presence of this competent, kind woman, who would stand in for her. She saw the doctor's wife as the silver lining of that depressing day. Under other circumstances, this joyful woman, wheeling the expensive pink car, would have been one of my mother's bridge friends. I could see them playing golf, having a Grasshopper at the club, shopping, wearing cocktail dresses with underskirts that rustled, and nodding in acquiescence and tolerance of their husbands. Both could have been accomplished, educated women in their own right, fully employed and successful, if they had lived and met just twenty years later. This was the close of the

1950s era of women as helpmates; they were all they could be. My mother and the doctor's wife held careful secrets and knew how to manage *difficulties* such as the one we were experiencing that day.

The pink Imperial's seats were a deep, amazing marshmallow leather, and the car was quiet and martini-chilled. I was frightened but tried not to show it, while my mother chatted for both of us—as if her daughter wasn't four months pregnant and going to hell instead of college. This first act of surrender, carefully orchestrated and justified, was only one step toward my redemption—unspoken but understood, and fervently prayed for by those in the know about my *troubles*.

My mother and the doctor's wife talked about the family I was about to join with a visitor's pass. There were five kids ranging in age from an infant girl to a boy only a few years younger than me. He attended a special Catholic boarding school for boys who wanted to become priests, which offered some assurance that I wouldn't be a near occasion of sin for the boy-priest on a daily basis. He would only be in residence in the family home occasionally. I sensed that the problem to be avoided was *me*, but I was overly sensitive to those insinuations.

We drove through charming old neighborhoods with a parkway dividing the boulevard, which was the landscape style my mother loved best. I could see her pull herself up a bit straighter as we swerved into the driveway of a house that occupied the best and highest lot of a broad cul-de-sac. The doctor's wife said that they had purchased all of the land in the neighborhood so only their friends could build homes there. Their house was bordered on one side by a cemetery. "Quiet neighbors," she laughed. More than two cars could fit in the garage with storage room to spare, and I was surprised by the built-in cupboards. Sharing a wall with the garage was the laundry room, which the doctor's wife described as "Missoura's domain—the Negro maid. She's here during the week; a woman to be reckoned with. . . " The centerpiece of the laundry room was an ironing board and another ironing mystery called a mangle.

"My husband likes his shirts done at home," she announced, "and also good for linens." She smiled at me as though the mangle and I might become acquainted in a special way.

Missoura's domain gave way to a magnificent kitchen, which was more like a General Electric Theatre stage set, and the opposite of the many rental house kitchens in which my mother and I spent endless hours fixing meals. Mom and I exchanged the *look* and said nothing that would disclose how impressed we were. Most astonishing to me was that the lower cupboard doors concealed the dishwasher, refrigerator, and a trash bin. Even I, a wayward teenage girl, filed away the elegance of that room for my future perfect house and my future perfect family with my future perfect husband.

Later, I would hear my parents discuss how *lucky* I'd been to end up with this lovely family. The truth was, I always felt lucky and never expected less. My attitude was shaped by my Oklahoma Nana's mantra—*You are special because your Dad died in the war*. A vague connection, of course, but my adopted father put it another way—*You always land in a pile of shit and come up smelling like a rose.* The message was clear that my parents considered my stay with the doctor's family a far better arrangement than my being doomed to a maternity home. Over time, I wondered with confusion why I wasn't sent to live with my

Oklahoma Nana in the house where I always slept in the sunniest corner bedroom, where she would fill the bathtub with bubbles, hold my hand as we walked to Woolworth's for lunch, and let me drink cocoa in her cozy yellow kitchen if I couldn't sleep.

I learned later that neither of my Nanas were told of my pregnancy nor were they consulted on possible solutions. Nana Lettie would have certainly wanted me to live with her forever and attend college in Enid, Oklahoma, where she lived. Her house was a safe haven, and the woman neither judged nor tolerated fools. She accepted her family with the kind of love that people only hope to receive. She would have handled my situation differently and would have made certain that I had a place at the deciding table. My Nana Nell, on the other hand, was Irish, and she would have probably suggested war with Joe's people and something worse for him. If I had been given an opportunity to live with one of my grandmothers, I would have been nurtured, sheltered, and released back into the world with more love and less shame.

Each room of the doctor's house was incrementally larger, more wood-paneled, held taller and larger windows, and more French doors than the last. The den, adjacent to the kitchen, was fully paneled in the same exotic pecan wood as the kitchen cabinets, which wrapped so completely around the room that the den could be mistaken for an extension of the kitchen itself. A color television, yet unknown in my parents' house, was set into a cabinet with doors, which remained closed unless the television was turned on. The television, I would soon learn, was completely controlled by the doctor, who would sit at his desk and change the channels by hand. Remote controls were still in the testing lab in 1963 along with birth control pills. This color television was larger than my parent's black and white model with a rabbit-eared antenna and was enough for me to be impressed, vowing to watch whatever was presented, without complaint.

We paid a cursory visit to the dining room, where I was told that dinners with all children present was the rule rather than the exception. I would soon learn that a popular main course in this household was well-done steak because that was how *the doctor* liked it. I almost threw up on the wool carpet at the thought of ever eating steak, no matter what its condition. I was a picky eater who preferred potatoes and bread for actual meals. When the first McDonalds appeared in our suburban neighborhood, I discovered French fries as a food group and considered myself an exotic vegetable eater. I decided I would play my *condition card* as needed in regards to food. It was ironic that later, deep into my pregnancy, I would crave meat—probably a result of the sheer number of steaks that were toasted black on the barbeque grill embedded in the stovetop. The restaurant-size cooking space included at least twelve burners and the mysterious grill mechanism that was hard to completely clean because of the charred flesh smell which lingered. The refrigerator in the doctor's house was a monument and could easily have held within itself the icebox kept on the back porch in my parents' first house in Minneapolis.

The doctor's wife described the living room as *sunken.* My mother and I smiled knowingly. We knew about *sunken* living rooms, since our current rental house had one, too. When the doctor's wife informed me that I could help *poor old* Missoura clean the several hundred squares of window glass in the living room and dining room once a month, I nearly jumped right through the panes. My mother changed the window-washing subject with the deftness of an assassin. I was expected to avoid argument or dismay and remain compliant and cheerful. This I knew with certainty. Any other behavior could result in being sent home, which would blow our cover story, contrived to fool no one, about my extended visit to my *aunt*.

The overhanging threat that would remain my constant companion was banishment or rejection. Unwed pregnant girls were perceived as *dangerous* and capable of anything, including random seduction and unexpected, rash behavior. After all, they'd had sex. To invite *these girls* into your home, as the doctor and his gracious wife did out of kindness and charity, was both risky and admirable. I wasn't the first, nor would I be the last unwed girl to enjoy their hospitality. They must have calculated the risk and then attached their exacting expectations. I learned that the unnamed girl, who had lived with them most recently, earned favorite status by helping out with housework, taking care of the kids, and other vague accomplishments, but primarily, she cooperatively and cheerfully surrendered her baby at the end of her stay. She was also older than me, and I was stepping into her place as the next girl to be helped out of a difficult and shameful situation. The expected behavior and end result was only part of the story and adaptation I would learn between my arrival at the doctor's house and February.

Off the den, sharing a wall with the doctor's

television, was *my* room. It was accessed through a separate hall door and occupied its private corner of the house. By anyone's standards, it was a cozy sanctuary. There was one double bed, not two narrow twin beds or bunk beds that I was accustomed to, and a private bathroom with a window. The scenery on that side of the house was a full-on view of the cemetery, which was fine with me, since the scenery matched my mood. I had two other windows, but the rows of ancient and recent tombstones would become familiar friends over the next few months. Later, I would discover that each stone held a story written between the dates that depicted a life barely lived or a century-long marriage of a couple who died together. Some graves were clustered in family groups, others stood alone as if they had lived that way, and all interested me for the story they did and didn't tell.

As I surveyed my new room, I noticed the built-in shelves, cabinets, and desk. I'd brought my portable record player because my music was essential, and I realized that it would fit perfectly on those shelves. Everything about the room was immaculate. As a girl with little inclination toward tidiness or fear of dust or clutter, I took the pristine state of that room as a forewarning. I sighed and wondered how I would get away with having a cigarette in there. I would have gladly lived only in that room until my mother came to collect me again, and indeed, I tried to do just that at the start of my *visit* with the doctor's family. That course of action failed, but this bedroom became a safe place for me during those months away from home.

The only other room, *a suite*, in that part of the house was the master bedroom. As a girl whose parents sometimes didn't have a bedroom for their tiny double bed, but slept instead on a pullout couch in the living room, a master suite with French doors, which led to a pool, seemed decadent and made the list for my perfect future house. I filed the idea away along with appliances shrouded behind cupboard doors, a restaurant-size dishwasher, a maid to iron my husband's shirts, and, of course, a pink car.

One glance at my mother, chatting like old pals with the doctor's wife, impressed me more than the unfolding layout of the house. I was in awe of her navigational skills and wished I'd learned her grace under pressure. Maybe if I were as skillful as she, I wouldn't be in this situation.

We continued touring the doctor's home, climbing a steep stairway that wasn't visible from the main floor but accessible through a door in the kitchen. This was the children's lair—three oversized bedrooms—one straight ahead and one on each side of a dividing hallway. The room of the two younger boys was on the left, the two girls shared a room at the front of the house, and the revered, eldest son's impeccable room was on the right, over the garage. They were dormer rooms with upholstered benches under the windows. I loved this style and regretted that my first-floor room had no window seat to overlook the cemetery. I could imagine myself like Jo in *Little Women*, curled up on snowy afternoons in a picturesque window.

One thing I would have added to the children's rooms was dark-blue ceiling wallpaper with silver stars, which glowed in the night. I often stayed in a tiny dormer bedroom at my Aunt Virginia's house, where stars shone above the bed—terrifying and fascinating in equal measure.

The carefully considered theme of the younger boys' room was cowboy chic—pseudo-saddles sewn into the genuine leather headboards, little spur table lamps, two matching rolltop desks, and a cowboy boot wastebasket. No boys' rooms in my experience had empty wastebaskets and such tidy beds. *Missoura, the maid*, I thought, *and now probably me in the role of housekeeper.*

The two girls shared an elegant 1960s Laura Ashley space. There was a single bed with a puffy floral duvet and matching pillow shams. A crib was nestled in the space where the window was built out over the front of the house. The baby and I shared the same view of the cemetery. I sighed as I thought of the crowded small room I shared with my sister, and our washable, green Sears' ripcord bedspreads my mother's budget allowed.

We glanced into the eldest boy's room, but not for long, as if it were a sacred space or shrine. The drapes were closed, creating a cool funereal absence, which piqued my curiosity about its occasional occupant. Books were arranged on an austere desk below a crucifix with crossed, crumbling palm fronds over the top. I knew the work of a Palm Sunday past. Nothing else might identify this as the room of a teenage boy who had already decided he would be a celibate priest for life. I took one last look and followed my mother and the doctor's wife back down the narrow stairs.

In the kitchen, there were kids everywhere, and the doctor's wife was delighted to see them after what was surely a calculated absence.

"Oh, look she's here—this is Shari and her mother." The doctor's wife introduced us to each child in turn, mentioning again the absence of the eldest. I don't think in retrospect that anyone curtseyed, but I can certainly imagine that it might have happened.

The children were polite, but unimpressed. At my house, a visitor would take their chances navigating the maze of my siblings' toys and blanket forts. Our black and white television was always on, and the phone rang more for my popular mother than it did for me. Nothing was where it belonged, which caused a low level of hysteria, except for the hour before my father came home from work. That was when we were transformed, as was our mother, into calm children and the waiting wife—our less privileged version.

"Daddy's home. Say hello and then go play—*quietly*," my mother would say. With certainty, my father had stopped at a local bar for a pre-arrival Manhattan or two, always made with cherries. At home we could count on sneaking maraschinos marinated in bourbon and vermouth. A pitcher of frosty Manhattans (about five glasses worth) was always waiting for him when he got home. Those cherries carried tacit permission for us to learn and enjoy the taste of alcohol no matter what our age. They were only *cherries* after all—a delicious precursor to something forbidden, like sloe gin.

My first dinner at the doctor's house was steak, baked potatoes, and some vegetable I wouldn't have normally eaten. There were also bland, white rolls, which I knew were my friend. I drank milk with the rest of the kids and was grateful for the comfort it provided. I realized that faking or having food aversion due to pregnancy might not work. At this point, I could have avoided meals altogether. My mother and I ate with the doctor's family in the dining room, where the lights were dimmed to adult-eating level. It was here that I became entranced with the baby girl, who sat in her pecan highchair between her mother and me in the seating place I would occupy for the next five months. At this first dinner, I would enjoy the last minutes of *guest* status within a family that would soon absorb me as their newest, visiting member.

Before I was ready, it was time for my mother to be taken back to the airport—without me.

"Well, honey, I need to get Shari's mother back to the airport," announced the doctor, who was going to drive her there in his beige Chevrolet Bel Air. I presumed he had things to discuss with her that would be far more somber than the bright conversation she had enjoyed with his wife. Mom spent most of our remaining time together thanking the doctor and his wife for their generosity, claiming that I would be a great help with the kids, promising that I would be no trouble, and that *the time would fly*. I know that my mother was avoiding eye contact with me, because when she finally turned around as I walked behind her, I sensed her difficulty in holding herself together—she was leaving her daughter with a family of strangers. I couldn't have known what this departure would cost her. She knew I would recover from the separation better than she would. If she were leaving me at college, it would be a different kind of departure, a socially acceptable one, and a better reflection upon her as a mother. My pregnancy was a terrible misstep, and as she acted out those final moments at the doctor's door, she became very fragile. While I would survive, a part of her would not. Something in my little mother would never rebound from the weight of having an unmarried pregnant daughter and the subsequent loss of her first grandchild. We lived in a society that demanded shame and penalty for transgressions; the sins of the daughter were the sins of the mother.

We hugged as long as my mother ever hugged anyone—a short definite squeeze. She blinked back tears, then out the door, abandoning me until next year. It was early fall, and I was expected to stay until February, the probable time I would give birth. I wanted to cling to my mother's coat and plead, "How can you be so polite to them when I am so terrified?"

I watched the Bel Air pull out of the garage, and I could see my mother lighting a cigarette from the doctor's lighter. The mask I wore at that moment was as fragile as my mother's bravado. I had failed to learn the level of stoicism which the women on my Irish side of the family tried to pass down. They were wrong. Suffering in silence wasn't noble. It could give one cancer as surely as slow poison or resentment. I watched the tailfin lights disappear around the cul-de-sac, and I went back inside to help with the dishes.

IV
Black Cherries Jubilee
Kansas City
1963 - 1964

Nothing about this solution for my pregnancy, no matter how civilized, felt fair or equitable to me—it was simply how such matters were handled in 1963. It wasn't enough that I was a rosary-praying, mass-attending, Catholic girl who was disciplined in all the rituals, language, and beliefs. The problem was that I didn't believe in the mystery any more. My life long acceptance of things on *faith* had become only *false evidence appearing real—F.E.A.R.* in its finest form. I was smothered in terror, and I had been abandoned by family, friends, and boyfriend, just as the baby, who rode small and silent within me, would be abandoned by his mother.

My busy, growing baby shared space with the dilemma I began to feel in the pit of my stomach, which I experienced in greater degrees as each month passed. Despite my difficult circumstances and the odd surreal expectations of polite society, my hormones were changing so that I would become a *mother*. Nothing could convince my body that it was only an incubator—minus the wires, pumps, and cold metal. I learned that *nature* wasn't discriminating, and I couldn't fool my hormones. My pregnancy thus far was normal, healthy, and progressing, as if in defiance of how inappropriate and insufferable my actions had been.

I began to understand that the price is paid, not only by the woman who gets pregnant, but ultimately by the child whom she is forced to leave. Only a few months before, I had celebrated my boyfriend's seventeenth birthday by having sex with him—the perfect gift. At that moment, I might have believed that my future husband *was* my boyfriend. Senses dulled by the elixir of sloe gin, perfunctory and insincere declarations of love, and the insistence that rubbers ruined it for guys, whatever *it* might be, I gave in and put out, and now here I was in Kansas.

All my friends were headed to college and my boyfriend had assumed radio silence. My birthday present to him had been the gift that kept on giving. I didn't get pregnant that night in the basement, but as a result of one of the innumerable times thereafter, which weren't necessarily predicated by anything except a strong desire to love and be loved.

Now, it was irrelevant, the where and when, but the math bore out my suspicions. There were only so many dates of conception if figured backward from the date of birth; I had seen the little wheel for that in the doctor's office.

I tried not to consider the outside world as I adjusted to life as the now-eldest girl in a larger, more devoutly Catholic family than my own. Everything about the doctor's household was expansive and generous. And, there was the swimming pool, though I wouldn't be living there during the summer. I didn't own a maternity bathing suit—I refused to even consider it.

The doctor and his wife were affectionate and forever kissing each other *on the lips* every time one of them arrived home or left the house. The doctor came home for lunch every day (big lip lock), read *Time Magazine* with a holy devotion, and smoked cigarettes while he ate. I learned how to make and serve his sandwiches, which earned me the right to listen and agree with him about local and world events. He was a Republican, like my parents, which I found comforting, maybe because I had listened to Eisenhower's election on my grandfather's radio. I hadn't yet begun to think for myself about politics, and this wasn't a good time to start.

Though I secretly feared him, I figured that being available for idle chat would please him and make it less likely that I might be sent away.

I'd only been there a month, maybe less (time had slowed to an infinitesimal creep), when I found a letter, torn to shreds, in the kitchen trash. Having a feeling that it was about me, I carefully collected the pieces and stashed them in my room. That night, while locked in my private bathroom with Barbra Streisand playing on the record player in my adjoining bedroom, *I stayed too long at the fair and down with love and flowers and rice and shoes*, I pieced together the discarded letter.

It had been addressed to my parents and detailed, for their reading pleasure, the many ways I wasn't making an effort to be a cooperative, cheerful, or functional part of their family. It spoke of my inherent laziness, and how I always wanted to sleep or read, how my somber attitude upset everyone, but worse, how I didn't anticipate what chores needed to be done without being prompted. I didn't take an interest in cleaning, and apparently, when I did clean something, it was a shoddy effort.

I recognized the handwriting of the doctor's wife. She wrote that they were considering sending me home. With cold fear, it occurred to me that though the letter had been discarded, it could have been a first draft or a failed effort. Perhaps another version hadn't been sent at all. Who could I ask? No one. It was bad enough that I was a girl who had sex, but now I was the girl who snooped through the garbage?

I opened the bathroom window, lit a contraband cigarette stolen from the doctor's pack, and considered my options. I was worried that I had disappointed the very people who were kind enough to keep my secret, but I was sad about being sequestered as a faux member of a family upon whom I had been foisted. The doctor was commended for taking in *girls like me*, and I was supposed to be grateful and nice. Now it seemed clear that I had failed, and I felt neither *grateful* nor *nice*. I continually thought about my boyfriend enjoying his senior year of high school, dating other girls, and I imagined that my friends' college lives were as perfect as mine was complicated. My choice was clear—I needed to improve my people-pleasing, good-girl attitude and become the best unwed mother they'd ever had in their house. At that moment, I wanted the next girl, who lived with the doctor, to hear about how wonderful *Shari* had been. She would feel pressure to live up to *my* example.

The next morning, I swooped into the kitchen, announced that I needed something to do, and though no one ever knew I'd found the letter, I became exactly what they wanted. I ignored my feelings and hatched a plan regarding my baby that I would realize eighteen years later. *This*, I thought, *was easy—I can be whoever they need me to be*. That was the role of a hostage, wasn't it? Decades later, when I learned about trauma bonding, I could relate. What I didn't know that day—my feelings for the family, especially for the doctor's wife, would become genuine and deep.

The younger kids and I became inseparable. I looked forward to them coming home each day from school so that we could play, go shopping, or just be silly together. The baby girl was constantly with me during the day, and I usually put her to bed at night. I carried her around like I had carried my three younger siblings, and in return, she made me laugh and wish that she were mine. This baby didn't know my story, and she accepted me for who I was—an amusing babysitter, who never said no to any of her demands.

The greatest joy of my social life was when the oldest son would come home from the seminary for a weekend. He was a freshman in high school, *much* younger than me, and admittedly, he had the potential to be cute. I would have died a terrible torturous death before admitting that I was attracted to him, since I had learned to be suspicious of all feelings. The unspoken coda was that if you were pregnant and unmarried, you were supposed to turn every thought and feeling inward. You could reclaim them later, like the wire basket at the public pool, where you entrusted your underpants and your dollar for a Holloway Sucker in exchange for a numbered diaper pin.

The oldest son seemed glad to have me living at the house, and our friendship was forged with an element of comfort and laughter, which I cherished. We talked about music, movies, friends (his), parents (his), and his experience in the pre-seminary program. Since I couldn't imagine life without a boyfriend, I asked him a roundabout question that addressed the issue of celibacy and girls—I knew I was treading on hallowed ground with combat boots, risking my reputation as a reformed *bad* girl by asking a pending priest such a bold question. Since everything was supposed to be accepted on faith in the Catholic Church, I wasn't surprised when he looked surprised and didn't have an answer to my celibacy query. *Was it possible*, I wondered, *that it hadn't crossed his mind yet?* He was a freshman that year, so maybe he hadn't started to think seriously about girls.

As a freshman in high school, I hadn't encountered the urges that drove me now. Of course, we never mentioned that I was pregnant nor what that implied about me. When his visit was over, and he returned to the seminary, I'd miss him—his tacit approval made me feel almost normal. I'm sure we were watched by the doctor and his wife, who worried that I might seduce their young virgin seminarian with my nefarious, seven-month pregnant ways. Misbehavior on my part wasn't an option, since I inhabited a body that now made my sins obvious. Also, I considered the eldest son a splendid temporary sibling, and I was still secretly yearning for Joe, my boyfriend.

My time in the doctor's home became sublime. I had figured out the puzzle of survival and had grown to love them all, even the doctor, who rarely smiled, but was monitoring my pregnancy and health with benevolence and care.

The holidays were pending, and I had grown accustomed to my place in the family as the temporary fake daughter. I also believed that the doctor and his wife were lucky to have me, and I vowed that when I had kids and needed extra help, I would put in for an unwed mother. Since the family didn't enjoy a major social life, I was always with at least one of them, and because I had no place to go outside of the house, I was always available for babysitting. In those months, we only went out once as a family—to *Man of La Mancha* in a downtown Kansas City theater.

Most mornings I attended mass, which was held in

the basement of the local Catholic grade school while a new church was being built through Sunday fundraising. The space, shadowy and impermanent like a typical school basement, provided the faithful with folding chairs. There were no kneelers so we had to kneel on the floor, and we faced an altar, which was only a table without a proper tabernacle behind it. Despite that, I found solace in that odd space for a church, and I loved my daily walk there, no matter what the weather might be. Going to mass was one of the few away-from-home trips which I was allowed to take. I was on a very short tether at the doctor's house, and as I walked, I was finally alone with my thoughts, which were often detailed fantasies of my reunion with Joe and that *clean slate* I was promised by my parents.

After a few months of living with the doctor's family, I earned a certificate from the executive secretarial program of The Kansas City School of Business. I was already a good typist, enjoyed taking Gregg shorthand dictation, and I thought about being a *Girl Friday*, as secretarial work was euphemistically called, to a handsome boss. I hoped that this training would be useful for my uncertain future, and importantly, it absorbed time, getting me out of the house on a sanctioned field trip every week.

Many afternoons and some evenings, I played chess with the young priest who was doing his rotation in the neighborhood parish. I wondered if he was doing charity work with me, but our friendship was based on the endless games I learned to win, and it provided a respite from everything else. I was relieved that chess wasn't a game that excluded pregnant teenage girls. The priest was a fine and patient teacher, whom I never saw again, but always wanted to thank for his kindness. He never made me feel that wave of shame that I sometimes felt from others.

I had also grown close to Missoura, the family's maid—she became a friend to me during this difficult time. She certainly worked around the doctor's house more than I did. As my child care duties permitted, or while the baby slept, I would assist Missoura doing whatever was on the household list or on the prescribed schedule for that day of the week. I did, indeed, wash those hundreds of panes in the living room windows—several times. Missoura would wash inside, and I washed outside or vice-versa. I often offered to work on the outside glass because Missoura said that the winter cold chilled her bones. I braved the weather, though by then, I was eight months pregnant. There were none of the restrictions on pregnant women that exist now. I was as hearty as the Irish-pioneer, breeding women before me. They had each managed to have at least four children, sometimes six, and there was never a whisper of complaint or warning about pregnancy being anything but a time of waiting for a baby to be born while one still worked each day. Who was I to mess with that kind of history?

From Missoura and the doctor's wife, I learned exactly how to fold mangle-ironed sheets within one another and to arrange them on the shelves of the deep linen closet, which was larger than my parents' entire bedroom closet. I decided I could do without a mangle on the growing list of the items which would assure my future domestic bliss. In a way, I was acquiring a discerning aptitude for true quality, good taste, and exacting order. I had the doctor's wife to thank for those lessons that I appreciate now, even though I still can't manage to organize my linens in a manner that would make her proud.

I had no personal interaction with the *mangle*, whose name alone was daunting. The pungent, starchy steamy smell it produced was imprinted on my brain. So was the smell of constantly brewing Folger's coffee and cigarette smoke. These odors were familiar to me as both had been part of the fabric of my life at home.

The doctor's wife was a gifted baker. She gave me a recipe for Rum Butter Pumpkin Cake, doused in potent, hot-buttered rum sauce, which she typed for me on a recipe card that I still own. Booze was part of our diet back then, and no one thought twice when alcohol was camouflaged in deserts as luscious as Cherries Jubilee. That awareness came gradually to society, but at that time, I was part of the cocktails-before-dinner generation.

I remained a poor eater, as my pre-pregnancy weight—barely above 100 pounds—would attest. I was skinny even while pregnant. Once as I walked to mass, boys in a car whistled at me. From the back, I realized that I was still *me*. Each day with the doctor's family, I feared that I might be sent home for refusing to eat salad with Roquefort dressing, my portion of the dreaded steak (charred and tough), or the vegetables produced in the restaurant-sized kitchen. I reluctantly learned to swallow, not to gag on, the food textures that were displeasing. I also took on the job of serving and allotting portions on everyone's plate. I set and cleared the table, then washed the dishes. By serving the food and cleaning up the table, I hoped that whatever was left on my plate would go unnoticed—a portion of steak, most of the salad with Roquefort dressing, the occasional Brussel sprout. For dessert, there was always Jell-O, which included floating fruit or a layer of applesauce, and plenty of Wonder Bread. I felt sorry for the baby within me, but these desserts were my dietary salvation.

I'm sure the doctor and his wife regularly assessed my attitude and progress behind the closed double doors of their master bedroom, but they were unprepared when I announced that I was thinking of *keeping this baby.* This was the first time I dared to call it what it was. I told them that I had begun having feelings, which I guessed were maternal. I'd lost all sense of reason or caution, and I wanted to explore this new idea with them. The doctor's response was based on enthusiastic promises he must have made to the adoptive parents and his assurance about the quality of *the mother.* These pending commitments, probably negotiated by the doctor himself, prompted his swift and stern response to me:

"If you plan to do that, you will have to leave immediately. There are people counting on receiving this baby, who would be far better parents than you could be at this time in your life."

I knew that I once again disappointed them and earned their disapproval. They had reminded me that I had no rights—my feelings were irrelevant and insincere. Perhaps, I was confused by my maternal hormones. I could only imagine the hushed pillow-talk between the doctor and his wife that night, as they spoke about how he had certainly *nipped that little problem in the bud.* I wondered why it was so shocking to them that I would have these feelings, and considering my compliance, why was it not commendable that I was brave enough to share what I felt?

My instant capitulation to the scolding I received explains why, in later years, I have never hesitated to ask for what I want, and why *No* means it's time for a new question. While I may not have always been pleased with my subsequent choices since then, at least they are *mine*. I was reduced to powerlessness that night, disallowed the expression of any feelings or opinions about *my* pregnancy.

Since then, I've fantasized what it would have been like to meet the adoptive parents, to take the measure of the people who wanted my child, to be given an opportunity to feel comfort, grief, or dismay. None of that was acceptable because we all lived in unspoken fear of losing something. The adoptive parents feared losing my child to some whim I might have, or they feared the possibility that my child could be handicapped in some way. Disability would have been a deal breaker, I was told. For the doctor and his wife, they might have lost faith in their ability *to do the right thing.* Looking back, I realize that an already difficult situation was made worse by everyone's good intentions. In social work school, I would learn about self-determination and how vital it is to the healing process. Maybe self-determination, like remote controls and birth control, hadn't been invented yet in 1963. Although I had dared to mention that I might want to keep my baby, I wasn't sent home.

What I loved best about living with the doctor's family was the sheer comfort and beauty of the place. It was a spacious home, full of matching burnished stuff—silverware, furniture, a mantle, crown molding and baseboards, built-in cabinetry, lush upholstery in the living and dining rooms, voluptuously tasteful drapery custom-made for the windows, dustless table tops with minimal ornamentation, except for a few religious icons. The white Pietà fascinated me as the idealized image of mother and child that would never be my experience.

One day, after helping the doctor's wife prepare lunch, I discovered the basement bomb shelter—definitely a privileged addition to upper-class homes, but not one my parents could afford or consider. We didn't discuss possible nuclear fallout or the threat of nuclear war in my family because it came too close to our emotional center. My biological father had been killed in war, and my second father had been wounded physically and mentally by his military service. The doctor's wife asked me to carry some canned goods into the shelter, which afforded me a glimpse of their certain survival plan. It was a basement room with a thick door and, I was told, reinforced walls. There were no windows, but by the vague light of the single bulb in the reinforced ceiling, I could make out shelves of camping supplies, cases of Coke, and a battery radio. The shelter was exotic, and for those months I lived above it, I was certain that I could survive any disaster—natural or manmade. It didn't look exactly comfortable, but I figured that a nuclear war would be brief and only the sheltered few would survive. I refrained from asking the doctor or his wife too many questions about this Cold War bunker in their basement. When I later suggested to my parents that my father could build one for us, my dad rolled his eyes, and my mom said that it would be a great weekend project for him.

This expansive house was made finer by the warmth of the doctor's wife, whom I admired and wanted to emulate. She was a fearless and highly skilled dessert maker, favoring complicated recipes, like Bananas Foster.

It was at her table that I had Cherries Jubilee for the first time—smooth vanilla ice cream melting under the cherries, which were hot, tart, sweet, and slightly drunk. She usually made this dessert when the oldest son came home, and it was a tiny, guilty pleasure for me of which I had too few. Her cooking compared well with my own mother's skill and imagination in the kitchen. I was dreading food less these days, which was an improvement. It was necessary for me to eat, since *this baby* was growing toward our ultimate escape in February.

On November 22, 1963, I went Christmas shopping with one of the children at the Country Club Plaza in Kansas City. We were having lunch at a cozy café when we heard the first announcement on the radio that President Kennedy had been shot and wounded while on a trip to Dallas. I reassured the doctor's young son, who seemed shocked, that the news report only said that the president had been *wounded*. Wounded was something a television-viewing, cowboy-loving public could understand. We finished our lunch quickly and called the doctor's wife from a ten-cent pay phone, asking her to pick us up; Christmas shopping had suddenly lost its cache. As we stood on the corner awaiting our ride, people were rushing past us, exclaiming that the president was dead—*assassinated*—a word I hadn't heard since writing an essay about President Lincoln in grade school.

Lincoln's assassination made historical sense, and most of us, in 1963, believed that we were safe in the United States of America, the country that won all wars, possessed all answers, and elected beloved Catholic presidents. The Kennedy assassination and the events that followed were the denouement in the movie of my pregnancy—the turning point after which everything becomes clear or gets settled.

We were quickly collected from the Plaza by the doctor's wife, our shopping forgotten, and returned home, where we gathered in the doctor's den. We remained there for the entire weekend, watching history unfold. From repeated confirmation that our young president was dead through the live shooting of Lee Harvey Oswald by Jack Ruby, we sat in silence, except for the doctor's occasional commentary, which we acknowledged as true and pertinent. All of this eye-witnessed trauma and tragedy was testimony to the resilience of my baby-in-utero, who remained unimpressed and busy. Maybe it was the suspension of routine, the need to gather in one room, the silence we held, the reverence with which we paid attention to whatever was presented to us on television—from crying newscasters to saluting little boys. These were definitive events strung together in a safe space, where I was included in grief and loss for the first time. I found myself suspended in disbelief and astonishment. As collective innocents without much cynicism, we had no reason to believe this was anything but a distant one-off tragedy. We agreed that we would probably never again see such violence in this county nor have it intrude upon our lives.

The doctor later ordered the Kennedy memorial book, *The Torch is Passed*, from a coupon in the Kansas City Star, promising photos of the assassination. When it arrived, I turned the pages with devotion and horror. It was the first time I had seen such blatant violence in a miniscule, black and white photograph. I couldn't quit thinking about the images; I stared at the still photos from the Zapruder film—Jackie crawling across the back of the moving limousine to retrieve her husband's brains. We were all beginning to move in lockstep toward a new level of fear and awareness.

One night during that dark weekend in the den, the doctor's wife decided we needed Cherries Jubilee. By then, I'd learned the required exactness of timing so that the ice cream and the black cherries (from a can) didn't become a hopeless puddle. We poured the cherry mixture, which included liquor, into the chafing dish, lit the fire from the little can of Sterno beneath, and sat in the den watching the world commemorate our president—bowls of hot and cold dessert in our laps. In their laps—mine had disappeared.

V

Violet Night

Kansas City

February 4, 1964

Though I knew this story would have an inevitable arc, the way it unfolded into the finale surprised me. The murder of a president, the revenge of a strip club owner, Thanksgiving, Christmas, New Year's Eve, swept through as harbingers of endings and change. Each was a one-off occasion I would never repeat in this house with my surrogate family. Being pregnant had become my new normal. Though I didn't exactly know how it might present itself, time with my baby was nearly over, too. In quiet defiance of what society dictated as *the best interest of the child,* a connection between my baby and me happened anyway. I was told that I was unready and unworthy to be a mother, but the bond I had with this baby, whom I would soon surrender, was real. Bonding wasn't supposed to be included in the tidy package I would soon deliver.

If I received any preparatory wisdom about what to expect when giving birth to a baby, it had no context. I had a promised date for *something* to happen that would grant me passage from this to that, but since I had not named or acknowledged any feelings around what I was about to experience, it remained invisible and unsummoned. Connection between the final rite of passage and the surrender of my child was held in a silent reality. Instead, I focused on how I would miss the doctor's wife and the youngest child, who was inadvertently the beneficiary of my sublimated maternal instincts.

Somewhere in the fifth month of our relationship in the shared space of my body, I'd started talking to this lively force who defined me so clearly. I wondered what would happen if I admitted how connected I felt, how protective, how deeply sorrow was imbedded in me. That sorrow would stand ready to fill the space left by the baby, whom I would never hold nor hear, and it would remain long after I left Kansas. My sorrow was deep violet, the color of the priest's vestments during Lent, when we mourned.

The date on the little wheel in the doctor's office arrived in a gloomy haze of snow and cold. All routines remained in place. The kids were at school, except for the baby, lunch for the doctor exactly at the same time as all days before, a forgotten *Time Magazine* discussion, afternoon chores, dinner preparation, clean up, and television. I listened to Barbra singing *Down With Love,* as I read myself to sleep. The wind whipped against the house foretelling the promised blizzard.

Sometime after midnight, I awoke feeling a low, insistent discomfort. I hadn't considered what to do when *my time* came. If I'd been told, I either forgot or was intent on keeping the baby with me as long as possible. I stayed in bed another hour or two considering my options, postponing the inevitable, unable to turn to my sleeping husband and say, "Honey, it's time!"

I'd never been in the doctor's bedroom when he was in it, and their door was always closed when they slept. Tentatively, I knocked. Silence. I knocked again and announced myself. The doctor came to the door and knew, before I did, that it was probably *time.* He took me back to my room, where he examined me. He told his wife, who was now standing at my side that we should get ready to go to the hospital.

I didn't think about who would take care of the children when we left for the hospital. The three of us (the doctor driving, his wife in the passenger seat, and me in the back) were soon navigating an intense snowstorm in the beige Chevrolet. No Pink Imperial for us that night—hard to say what childbirth might have done to those marshmallow leather seats.

We were dropped off at the emergency entrance, and the doctor's wife pushed the requisite wheelchair settling me in a labor room.

"Remember," she said, "labor means work, not pain." Somehow her words comforted me. I was in labor a mere hour and a half before I was wheeled to delivery. It wasn't terrible, but it was odd to have everyone focused on the events between my legs. I was still modest and naïve about these things.

I was taken to a delivery room where the doctor appeared at the foot of the table on which I had been placed. The lights were glaring, intrusive, and hot. The room itself was frigid. My teeth were chattering, my legs felt otherworldly, and almost at once, a mask was put over my face.

I heard the doctor say to the anesthesiologist, in his commanding tone when he wanted the kids to behave at home, "Put her all the way down, so she doesn't hear the cry."

I woke up in the room where I had been with the doctor's wife. She was still there, as was the doctor, who was writing something in a chart. One of them told me that I had a perfect baby boy, and he had red hair just like mine.

I realized immediately that I'd never sit or walk again, which I figured was the penalty for having sex before marriage. Carol Burnett was dancing on the hospital television and as I watched her, I wondered how she could still dance after having *her* kids. In the early 1960s, new mothers were treated to indignities without apology. Prior to delivery, there was a complete shaving of the offending area near the baby's exit, accompanied by an enema to prevent any unpleasant and unsterile events. Post-delivery, my breasts were bound to stop milk flow; I was given tiny pills to contract my uterus, so much so that I thought another baby might be forthcoming. There was a heat lamp for stitches and something euphemistically called a sitz-bath, which did relieve whatever happened down there, causing me to feel so ruined. And what was worse—I was instructed not to go anywhere near the nursery.

Then, as now, the verboten fascinates and challenges me. In short, I enjoyed all the consequences of labor and delivery, with no reward. The memory of my mother's three babies dying just after their births crossed my mind. My mother had told me that she knew the babies were dead when the nurses closed her hospital room door. *She* probably didn't go to the nursery either. *Was this like having a dead baby*, I wondered, *and should I act a certain way?* At least I was spared a joyful, new-mother roommate, which I noted and appreciated. I imagined that maybe I didn't have a roommate because I was still considered toxic due to my sin.

On my second day in the hospital, a priest came to visit, and he admired the Sterling roses, the hard-to-find violet variety that the doctor and his wife had sent. I was still a devout Catholic girl, which hadn't changed, though I prayed mostly that I wouldn't go to hell.

The priest, wearing a narrow purple stole and bringing me Holy Communion, regarded the flowers and said, "Your husband must be very proud."

I replied, "Um, I don't have a husband. I am an unwed mother."

He looked as horrified to hear it, as I was to say it for the first time. He stammered something about being unable to give me Holy Communion as he backed out of my room.

To say that my devotion to my church suffered in his denial of my favorite sacrament (I never missed confession) would underestimate the impact of shame. I told the doctor's wife about the priest's refusal when she came to see me, and she was furious. Since women had no voice in patriarchal church matters, she promised to tell her husband. I never saw the priest again nor was I offered Holy Communion for the duration of my stay.

On the last night of the three days I was obligated to remain in the hospital (unlike the three-week stays of my mother's era), I decided to go to the nursery. It was late, visiting hours were long over, and the halls were dim and quiet. I'd heard and watched nurses push bassinets pass my room, so I knew which direction to take. I slowly navigated the route, fearing each moment that I would be caught and sent out into the night. I shuffled in the right direction, finding the window I sought. Only a few babies had been born that cold week, and they were arranged in two symmetrical rows by the window. I searched for the telltale, red-haired baby. How many could there be? In the few minutes I had to scan the sleeping or fist-waving, swaddled infants, I didn't see one that looked like me.

A nurse suddenly appeared and turned me away from the window, admonishing me for being near the nursery. She told me in a knowing voice that not all of the babies were on display. *As if,* I thought, *they hide the "illegitimate"* so they don't unduly influence the other *infants.* Were the only babies in the window, the ones with two married parents? I wondered whom they were protecting. I dared not ask to see my son.

Since there was no way to fight to see my baby without actually making a scene, I shuffled back to my room. Besides, it would be risky to make demands since being compliant was part of my cover story. I watched all the other mothers shuffle, and I thought shuffling was another unspoken rule. Banning me from the nursery window made perfect sense if the goals were to *forget* and *put it behind you* and *pay for your mistake* and *don't ask questions.* It was feared that once a baby was seen or held by the unwed mother, the adoption would be in jeopardy. Even then, I saw this logic and all that preceded it, as counterintuitive, but I had an obligation to my unseen unheld child, whom I fervently believed would be better off without me.

It wasn't popular and acceptable to talk about grief or deep feelings until the advent of talk shows in the 1980s. Something was driving me to try to see my son. I told myself that I only wanted to be assured that he was okay, but it was not my intent to disappoint or deny his new parents their/my child. What if I'd asked to hold him, to spend time with him, to kiss his sweet face, to inhale his baby smell, to say good-bye? This never would have happened because I was disconnected from my feelings, and I believed that I had no right to them, no right to ask for anything regarding my baby. All of that was more honest and instinctive than this forced course of action. I decided that since this was an exercise in deception, I could hold some secrets of my own from that moment forward.

I returned to the doctor's house and sat at the family table for the last time. My parents were there and our reunion had been muted. They looked worried about me as they assured me I would fly home with them that afternoon. My father was in charge of me again, but in a new way. He looked sad as well as determined. I'd only seen him look like this when he built the three tiny caskets in which he would transport my mother's dead babies from Minneapolis to St. Cloud, Minnesota, where they were buried in the family plot. Cemeteries were a recurring theme in our life.

The social worker had arrived, and it seemed that she'd been there before. She stayed bundled up, never removing her coat and refusing the doctor's offer of coffee, as though this was an odious but necessary break in her day. She clung to her many folders like they were endangered children and perhaps they were. From the closely held files, she extracted one that she named, *the final papers*. I wasn't asked anything nor were the papers explained to me in any detail. It was like many other parts of my life, where the adults knew the whole story and I knew only the title, but not the plot nor the ending. I knew that I was expected to sign these *final papers* in order to erase all that had transpired in the past nine months. The papers were my return ticket back to the life I'd been yearning for and imagining.

In what seemed perfunctory and expectant of the right answer, the social worker asked me, "Is this what *you* want to do?" No one had explained to me what *this* was nor did anyone ask how I was feeling. No one seemed to wonder if I truly understood the consequences of giving away my child. I must have said *yes*. The social worker, who was probably overheated in her coat by then, wrangled a chewed pen from the depths of her bag.

As I signed away my son, I thought, *I can't upset the kids with whom I've been living for the past months by refusing to put my signature on the paper and bringing the wrath of the doctor upon me.* Everyone seated at that table, except for me, believed this was the right decision, that justice had been served, a price had been extracted for sins committed, a baby would be better off, and life could be resumed without looking back.

I signed the paper under unseen and unspoken duress. Without the benefit of counseling, consulting, or gentle guidance, I knew only to maintain the compliance that was crucial to my survival. The only choice I had been given, coupled with my belief that this was the best and right thing to do, enabled me to sign my name, though I didn't fully understand what *final papers* meant. I fervently believed that my son would be better off with a set of chosen parents, not with a girl who hadn't yet figured out how to be an adult.

It felt too late for rebellion, so I set my shoulders back in the way my father had taught me. It demonstrated both strength and good posture. I hadn't seen my parents in five months, and I wanted them to be proud of me, so I didn't want to appear to question their decision regarding the adoption. I didn't cry then or for many years because the right to grieve had also been rescinded. My rights were non-existent at this moment, but my signature was imperative. As I signed, I felt as detached, disbelieving, stunned, and as confused as I did when President Kennedy was killed. What everyone saw was a new version of myself, the one who survived with dignity and cooperation.

I signed my son away to the collective relief of my

parents, the adoption worker, the doctor and his wife, and to the adoptive parents who took my son to their home that day to begin his new life. Maybe I briefly considered rebellion and a long-overdue fit of unleashed power somewhere between my first and last name. What I dared not tell was that I had fallen in love with that baby boy, who might be wondering with some infinitesimal remnant of our shared DNA, where his mother was. I knew not to dissent as I heard fair warning from the social worker that this was *final* and *irrevocable*. Neither of my parents asked to read what I was signing. We read nothing, we asked nothing. I looked only at the doctor's wife, who nodded and kept her hand on the back of my chair.

So, this was *giving away* a baby? Suddenly, the last nine months had gathered behind the curtain of then and now. Now my parents were going to take me home to my real life wherein I could exhale and walk again in my own footsteps, not in those of a girl banished for a misstep, not a murder. Did signing those papers compensate for anything? To whom did I owe this debt? To my parents for our shared pain and loss? To the doctor and his wife for their kindness? To the unknown, adoptive parents who hoped for a daughter? To my lost son, as assurance of his escape from an inadequate mother? To my boyfriend who'd escaped it all? To the people to whom I lied about the gap in my life, saying I had a lengthy visit with an aunt? To my grandmothers who were denied the truth and the chance to offer a kinder solution, maybe coming up with a way to keep their great-grandson and their granddaughter together? To my church and society that shamed me with a puritanical, archaic, judgmental solution to a problem, which would soon be a non-issue for single, pregnant movie stars and most other women by the time my child was an adult?

I left the doctor's house that day with my parents, my two Barbra Streisand albums, a certificate that qualified me to work as an executive secretary, and a semblance of who I'd been when I got there. I fell into the warm embrace of the doctor's wife, hugged the doctor briefly, and kissed the kids. I felt like crying, but my feelings and reactions had been too far repressed for too long to cry with conviction. In truth, I felt very little, but I knew that this was the final effort I could make for the family who had taught me so much, like how to fold sheets, make Cherries Jubilee and Rum Butter Pumpkin Cake.

My parents were my ballast in the pink Imperial, which returned me to the airport and toward re-entry into my preserved life. I returned to a different and much smaller rental house. *Getting away from those memories*, I heard my parents say when I shouldn't have been listening. I shared a room with my sister who was young and had remained oblivious to the reason for my long absence. My father drove us home from the airport that night in his beige Chevy Bel Air, and I marveled at the irony of coincidence. As though I had never been away, I slipped into my bed by the window, my little sister already asleep. None of my siblings were there to greet me, probably by design, nor did I ask my parents what they told them about my absence. My brother, Mark, was in bed, too, because he had a paper route and had to get up before dawn. My youngest brother, Tommy, was not yet five.

I returned to a silent and strange house where I could only surmise where everything had been placed after the recent move. My parents didn't seek change—

décor was inconsequential, furnishings were brown, the flowers and plants were plastic. After the doctor's plush home, everything here felt sad, even though I was finally home and out of my pregnancy jail. Long repressed thoughts of college life re-emerged as I realized I had other options as opposed to living the life of my parents.

As I slipped between the cool clean sheets on my twin bed, I felt free. I vowed never to do anything again that would confine me. With the smallness of this house, I felt that I was already growing again into my true self, the hidden girl, the person I lost for a while, like a magic sponge that becomes a new shape when water is added. This return home was water, and I was filling with hope.

Then and later, no one ever mentioned where I had been or asked what had happened to me there. I spoke about the doctor's family for a while, as though they were friends I'd met on a trip. Mom was polite and mildly inquisitive, but I soon realized it wasn't a popular topic. I summoned the secret silence I learned at the doctor's house and used it in reverse. I missed my surrogate family, but had no way to say it without hurting my mother's feelings. I had learned, after all, how *not* to say things, and it was clear that talk of them only threatened the fragile peace we had reestablished since my return. My siblings never mentioned my absence, though my brother, Mark, told me years later that he suspected the reason for my long trip.

I was an imposter on another level, a vision of innocence as was expected of me again, the lie morphing into a new reality. Within a week, I had fully extricated myself from my temporary identity within the doctor's family, and was thinking seriously about how I could *accidentally on purpose* run into Joe.

VI

Silver Star

Des Moines

1964

In the early 1960s, there was *going away to secretly have, then surrender a baby*, and there was *returning home afterward*. It was an inelegant departure, shrouded in strict, cruel secrecy and smothered in lies and evasions. The return home was accounted for with a vague reference to visiting somewhere else for approximately seven months. The only person I felt accountable to and whom I trusted was my friend, Carolyn, who had gone to college with her car. She came home on weekends and when we met again, I concocted a fable akin to unwed pregnant women whose cover story was that their "husband" was in Vietnam. My tale went like this:

"Joe and I got married, just to give the baby a name, and then we got an annulment."

I'd actually heard stories of illusory marriages that supposedly legitimized children. Telling Carolyn that Joe and I had gotten married only to surrender our child for adoption was the alternative to telling her nothing. Also, I wanted her to think that Joe *would* marry me, since this was part of my personal mythology. For some reason, I couldn't lie to Carolyn about not having that baby, not in light of the intense experience I had so recently survived, how I was yearning for my baby's sweet presence, how I was marking time along with his life in a distant place, where he lived with his new parents.

"The baby is with a nice Catholic family," I surmised, "and this is for the best. Imagine *me* as a mother!"

Carolyn didn't disagree with me, but she looked sadder than I dared to be. I had helped my mother raise my younger siblings since I was seven years old, and I would have made an excellent mother with some help and encouragement. I could have gone to college, found work, and had a full life of a different kind. But, not in 1963, when giving away a baby to strangers was preferable to keeping that baby with the woman who grew him under *her* heart.

Barely two weeks after my return from Kansas City, I told Carolyn the story of my faux marriage on our way to a party where I knew Joe might show up. It was Friday night, and some things never change. Enough people knew I'd returned from wherever they thought I'd been, and I was sure he had heard about my reappearance. The drama, the mystery, the bravery of simply showing up to the party was exciting. I was surprising even myself.

My mother handed over her Younkers charge card with which I bought an expensive—*twenty dollar*—baby-blue, angora sweater. I wore it that night because I knew blue looked fantastic on me. It was an airless hot sweater with flying fur. I sat on the couch facing the front door as we all drank Coke from small sea-green bottles. We were listening to a guy's story about someone finding a severed finger floating in a Coke, and he was holding up his bottle to the light, inspecting it, when the front door opened. Some people rushed in from the cold, as if they were falling out of a clown car. I saw Joe among them, but pretended I didn't by focusing on the guy who was still talking about cutoff fingers floating in soda pop. I wanted to look enraptured, but my heart was pounding. I expected Joe to see me and: a) be aloof, b) ignore me, c) be with some other girl, or d) all of the above, especially the *other girl* part.

Instead, he purposefully made his way toward me and held out his hand, saying, in the way I still found irresistible and for which I'd waited seven months, "Come with me." I did.

We ended up in a bedroom where he held me for a long time as he cried. He said that he wondered what had happened to me, and he hated not knowing where I was. He tried to offer an assortment of excuses as to why he never tried to inquire about my whereabouts. His apparent concern for me—full circle from the guy who wouldn't take my calls seven or eight months ago—was astonishing, but not unwelcome.

He seemed to step magically into the role of *my partner* in the pain, deep loss, confusion, and coercion that defined my absence. I was desperate for this validation, despite the too-little-too-late futility of his words. I wanted to believe that he did feel puzzlement and sorrow when I left, but these expressions of shared pain were impossible to square with the truth—Joe could have found me if he'd truly desired to rescue me. I was only in Kansas, one state away, nowhere exotic or untraceable.

Until that moment with Joe, I hadn't allowed myself any feelings outside of the line drawn for me by society and the adoption worker. I still believed that I had no rights, no voice, no opinion, no options, and certainly, no power. I would spend a lifetime countermanding all those dictates and deconstructing the mores that held women captive to the puritanical notion that young mothers without husbands are somehow inadequate.

I said aloud for the first time, "We have a son."

There were phrases I could have added that were attached to the forced surrender of a child: *He's better off, I wasn't ready to be a mother*, *No man will marry me if he knows I've had sex,* or translated differently, *Why buy the cow if the milk is so cheap?*

After that night, Joe and I became inseparable again. It was as though we could erase the time I spent in Kansas and the pregnancy. He was finishing his senior year in high school, and we vowed never to be separated again—there was no caution. Birth control was still unobtainable, except for the same method we had employed nine months prior.

We didn't initially tell our parents that we were together again. We feared their intervention, and we knew their success at keeping us apart. I figured that if I became pregnant again, Joe and I would simply get married.

When my parents eventually found out about our renewed relationship, they seemed more resigned than protective. I broke the news to my mother over our morning cigarette chat before I left the house for my temp job. I tried and failed to sell her on my certainty that this time, Joe and I would be together *forever*. The reaction of Joe's parents wasn't memorable—they always seemed to indulge him, and my pregnancy hadn't inconvenienced his family's life at all. We had cast our fates to the wind, and on some level, we believed that we had little to lose.

My mother—my adored mentor—would often proclaim her wisdom by telling me something terribly adult in a conspiratorial manner. I saw her talk to my father that way, to her bridge girlfriends, and to her sister, Madge, in Iowa. There was a certainty about her declarations, which were firmly based on some serious research in *Time Magazine* and the philosophical reading she enjoyed: Teilhard de Chardin's *The Phenomenon of*

Man, Robert Ardrey's *African Genesis* and *The Territorial Imperative*, Ann Morrow Lindbergh's *Gift from the Sea,* and Charles Goren's *Essentials of Contract Bridge*.

This was 1964, decades before the advent of self-help or support books, support groups, television psychologists, magazine articles that went beyond housekeeping and husband pleasing. What had occurred in my life was a giving in to one of the seven deadly sins—*lust*. There was no open dialogue or discussion about it, only repentance and atonement were allowed. I had received what I had deserved, and there would be no *dwelling on the past*, no rights granted for grief, and no allowance for magical thinking about the baby being *mine*.

My mother had been giving the possible backlash some thought. After I had admitted to her that Joe and I were in the middle of a relationship do-over, she later said, "Well, honey, that's your choice, but you two have no future. If you've had a baby and given *it* up for adoption, you and Joe can't marry with that loss between you. It would never work."

My mother wasn't the only one who'd been doing some deep thinking as I had come up with my own theory on the subject. She must have known what she was talking about, since she and my adopted father had four babies who died at birth or shortly thereafter. Their marriage wasn't so great—fraught with tension, my father's alcoholic rages, and my mother's silent long-suffering. I know now that her dire prediction didn't hold up for every couple who married each other after surrendering their first child for adoption. I have felt a certain level of envious respect for men and women who found each other again, dealt with the pain of that separation, searched for, then found their lost child, and integrated him or her with his or her true siblings.

On my nineteenth birthday, in an act that my parents believed was born of pure guilt, Joe gave me a Lindy star sapphire ring at a surprise birthday party he had planned. I thought the blue center stone matched his eyes, and the tiny diamonds surrounding it were proof that he loved me. Deep within the stone was the illusion of a perfect star—a hologram, something elusive, mutable, and visible only if held in a certain light. It was the metaphor for our relationship.

When I told Joe how much I adored the ring and that my mother had warned it was a guilty gesture, he looked at me a long while and said, "She could think that, but she'd be wrong." Our passion coupled with our shared, postpartum grief lashed us to the bow of a certain, sinking ship.

My resourceful parents were lobbying in a fierce manner for the day I would leave for Colorado and attend college in the fall. I imagined that were saying rosaries like crazy, counting down the days and nights each time I skipped out of the house into Joe's white convertible.

I believed that if Joe and I were meant to be together, nothing would interfere. The memory of being banished to Kansas, and the still-delicious feeling of freedom and possibility now that I was home, kept me in check. We knew the summer would end and that I would be the one leaving *him* this time. There was a power in that fact. His college plans were vague, and he was uncertain about his path and his future. How could I know that I was already moving out of our cozy sphere of young love and into a more expansive world?

Somehow among the shadowy, indeterminate standards of parenthood, my mother and father knew that time and space would provide the relief they needed from my obsession with this relationship. They probably hoped that history wouldn't repeat itself in the interim, because the outcome might be exactly the same—another extended trip visiting an "aunt." But Joe had convinced me that he was in this relationship for equal measure.

I had been given a full college scholarship to the Tobe Colburn School of Fashion in New York because of my Teen Board contributions to a column in *Seventeen Magazine*. If I had been able to accept this financial reward, I would have lived in the Barbizon Hotel in New York City, but the scholarship was only offered if I agreed to attend the school during the first semester after high school. In the fall of 1963, I wasn't studying the latest clothing trends—I was in Kansas.

As I read the shiny hopeful brochure of Loretto Heights Women's College, an elite Catholic school in Colorado, I noticed that it had an ambitious ski program. I had been a skier since childhood, and I was delighted to learn that the progressive feminist nuns, who lived and taught there, often skied with their students on weekends. All of the nuns I had known throughout grade school and high school merely glided on a track between convent, classes, and mass. The idea of *skiing* nuns was incomprehensible and irresistible. Skiing nuns, in addition to a horse stable, art studio, an architecturally stunning theatre, and an all-boys college down the road, prompted me to say to my mother, *Sign me up!* She wrote a check for $4,000 from my war-dead father's trust fund for the first two semesters. My new life had no price too high. My parents were willing to bet that I'd take one look at the Rocky Mountains and leave the folly of my ways behind in Iowa.

On the night I took the train from Des Moines to Denver, Joe came over to say good-bye. We stood at the front door in a melancholy embrace, despite the excitement about my college adventure.

Joe said, "You're a smart girl. You'll be great." While those words would foreshadow a distant possibility, I wanted to hear him say, "I will love you forever and never forget you."

All the way to Denver that night I stared at my Lindy star sapphire ring and its holographic silver star, and I felt free for the first time in my life. While on the train, I learned that at dawn, stars fade and a new light illuminates the mountains in a most hopeful way.

I had brought with me a book of Lord Byron's poetry, which contained a poem that reminded Joe of our relationship:

Stanzas Written on the Road Between Florence and Pisa

Oh, talk not to me of a name great in story;
The days of our youth are the days of our glory;
And the myrtle and ivy of sweet two-and-twenty
Are worth all your laurels, though ever so plenty.

What are garlands and crowns to the brow that is wrinkled?
'Tis but as a dead flower with May-dew besprinkled:
Then away with all such from the head that is hoary!
What care I for the wreaths that can only give glory?

O Fame!—if I e'er took delight in thy praises,
'Twas less for the sake of thy high-sounding phrases,

Than to see the bright eyes of the dear one discover
She thought that I was not unworthy to love her.

There chiefly I sought thee, there only I found thee;
Her glance was the best of the rays that surround thee;
When it sparkled o'er aught that was bright in my story,
I knew it was love, and I felt it was glory.

Part II

Anything that works against you
can also work for you
once you understand the Principle of Reverse.

—Maya Angelou

VII

Gold Rush

Chicago / Indianapolis

1979 - 1982

One of the best things about living in Chicago in 1979 was *The Phil Donahue Show,* televised from a downtown studio. Donahue, as he was known by his fans, was the talk show that started it all. Before video recording or television-on-demand, stay-at-home mothers watched shows in real time. High technology back then was ordering a transcript of a television program by phone, paying a fee, and waiting three to six weeks to receive it in the mail. It was thrilling.

Six years earlier, and ten years after my teenage pregnancy, I married the man I considered my soulmate. In 1973, finding your soulmate was essential, as it was believed that one perfect companion existed for everyone. I believed that my mother's soulmate was my birth father, who had died in World War II, just before I was born. She called her second husband, my adoptive father, her best friend, so I knew the difference. My mother didn't hold the ideal partner theory in high regard, saying that a couple needed to be friends first, as friendship was the only part of a marriage that survived. Still, I knew I'd found my soulmate no matter what she believed.

I met my husband, Paul, in 1972, and he was the first person with whom I felt comfortable enough to share the story of losing my baby to adoption. He gathered me up in his arms and told me that it didn't matter, that he loved me, would always love me, and he asked, "What can I do to help you with this?" I thought, *Only a soulmate could be that accepting*.

By 1979, we had a three-year-old son and two daughters, ages nine and eleven. I could watch *The Phil Donahue Show* five days a week if I planned play dates, aerobics, my part-time travel agency job, and tennis matches exactly right. On one particular day, Donahue announced that the topic of his show was adoption. My small son was playing with his Fisher Price airport, which included a big white jet with tiny places for the toy pilot, passengers, and luggage. His usual soundtrack as he played involved flying noises from a baby cockpit and an imagined, fighter pilot dialogue. The toy figures tumbled from baggage trucks and tiny bags were pushed up a fake ramp into the belly of the big plastic plane. My son was good at playing alone, but never strayed far from me as I did my various household tasks.

Donahue's guest on this day was Lee Campbell— a handsome, certain, *assertive* (an admirable, new quality for a woman), well-spoken individual, who was a BIRTHmother. *A what?* Lee had *surrendered* (not *given away* and she was very clear about the difference) her son, Michael, for adoption sixteen years prior. Never accepting what she had been forced to do and never forgetting this loss, she had created an organization for BIRTHparents.

Lee Campbell spoke for an uninterrupted twenty minutes about searching for and finding Michael. She recounted their first meeting at his adoptive parents' home as if it were completely normal to break the rules, to dare to ask, to reverse time. When she and Michael met, he greeted her by saying, "Hello again."

For the first time in sixteen years, I cried for the son whom I had been forced to surrender. I cried for Lee Campbell and Michael and for what my son and I had lost. I had never allowed myself to plumb the depths of those long-buried feelings because I didn't believe I had a right to feel anything. Lee Campbell had just told me otherwise. Some things, like surrendered babies, are seared into your mind because there is no forgetting in spite of societal insistence to the contrary.

I sat on the coffee table holding a dust cloth and a small boy who had fled his toy airport to save his mommy. He snuggled in my lap and offered me a pilot and a baggage cart. As I held him, I watched Lee Campbell and Phil Donahue adjust my course and change my life.

I had resolved to feel only mild curiosity and a fleeting sadness on each anniversary of my surrendered son's birth. That practice, however, did not protect me from the flood of grief that was triggered as I witnessed another birthmother speak about our mutual sorrow. I learned that Lee Campbell's organization, Concerned United Birthparents (CUB), was accessible to me for $15 and the courage to *out* myself as a former unwed mother. In exchange, I could find support among other women (and a few men who called themselves BIRTHfathers) who shared my lived experience.

I understood that day that I had *never* been alone. There were other birthmothers out there, in various levels of grief and anguish, searching for and wondering about *their* surrendered children. We were intertwined by our shared history, and we had each held a carefully guarded story that we attempted and failed to forget. Unreasonably, society had dictated the need for secrecy with a tenacity that wasn't easily broken. A birthmother's story was intended to be a secret forever, never spoken or acknowledged—*for the good of the baby*. And the baby, if referred to at all, was forever known as *that baby*—no fully-formed identity. Lee Campbell challenged this system of secrecy and shame by coming forward into the bright public forum of a television studio in Chicago to dispute the flawed thinking, which had denied birthmothers so much.

As if receiving long-awaited permission, with my young son playing on the floor with his toys, I broke through the yellow danger tape of my shame. I moved away from the ranks of silent, victimized women. Lee Campbell spoke to me in a way that imploded all the resolve, denial, and sorrow I had maintained as a barricade between the truth and myself. Immediately, I sent in $15 for a CUB membership application, gaining tacit permission to explore my trapped feelings and submerged desire to know my surrendered son. At that moment, I joined the gold rush for truth and information.

I had a revelatory experience while watching Donahue that day, and I explained it to my husband, "I only want him to know where to find me."

Though I wanted him to believe me, I knew I was deluding myself. There were so many more reasons why I believed that my first son should know me, including why I needed to know him. I soon began to tell people that I had four children. In practicing the truth, I hoped it would self-actualize.

One of the first people I told about my phantom son was my friend, Denise, who lived across the street in a mirror-image townhouse in a mirror-image young marriage with two boys who were friends with my two girls. I knew she would not judge me—she had been pregnant when she married just out of college. Denise had better timing and a fully-realized man who loved her. She was happy for me far beyond what is required of a good friend, and she validated my need to know about my son.

As a member of Concerned United Birthparents, I started working for the cause of adoption reform and birthmother support. I met with other birthmothers, talked to them on the phone, and wrote them letters. And while my involvement grew, so did the certainty that I would meet my son—it was only a matter of finding those breadcrumbs I'd left behind in the Kansas forest sixteen years earlier. I was mindful, however, of the witch that was Kansas adoption law and how she might steal me, then throw me in the oven. Through my involvement with CUB, I was learning that the terms, *real mother* or *biological mother,* were unacceptable terms for *birthmother.*

In associating with other birthmothers, I soon understood how difficult it was to approach the closed Kansas adoption system and how impossible it was to open sealed adoption records. There was a dire need for reformed adoption laws. In fighting for this cause, I volunteered to be the legislative reporter for CUB, and I wrote a column in their monthly newsletter, *The Communicator.* My affiliation with CUB enabled me to testify before legislators and other political groups, allowing me to identify as a birthmother who was disparaged by a punitive system, which denied my child access to vital information. Often the legislative panels, which dealt with adoption laws, were loaded in the favor of the adoption status quo, consisting of adoptive parent legislators or strict Catholics. I was the lone birthmother thrust into their midst. They smirked at my story and shook their heads in disbelief, though it wasn't clear to me why they seemed so negative and dismissive. In spite of this reaction, CUB sent me to these panels in order to raise consciousness, armed with the courage of my birthmother convictions. It was while attending legislative groups, perhaps more than anywhere, that I planned an insurrection against this archaic institution. I, like my red luggage, might be tossed around plenty, maybe run over, but I would never break open.

If adoption laws were reformed, my son would then have access to the truth about his family history. Much had changed since I was eighteen years old. The information the adoption agency included in an adoptee's file was a vaguely defined fiction—a reflection of what adoptive parents wanted to believe—those things that placed the birthmother in the best possible light. It was important to portray her as coming from a religious and intact family, possessing a job or an education, having excellent mental and physical health, and if possible, to portray her as the daughter of a doctor, university professor, or other professional. Above all, the birthmother must be Caucasian with no questionable bloodline. And paradoxically, this same pregnant woman was also customarily banished in shame and despair.

In the adoption file and on the original birth certificate, the birthfather was only alluded to, yet he was given all the same glowing attributes as the birthmother, maybe more. Rarely was he named. If he were labeled *unknown*, this gave the birthmother the added cache of being a possible *tramp*. Most birthfathers were protected with unknown or withheld status—unidentified because they were sometimes married, which granted justification for making a mother and baby disappear. The reasons for protecting the birthfather conspired to vilify the birthmother, and this in turn, exonerated him. If the birthfather of my son had been a person of color (as the social worker had asked my mother), then my son would have had little chance of adoption. It is no wonder that an inconvenient scandal of this kind is best rectified by giving away the child to someone of better moral means—only if the child is "perfect," of course. All of this creative misinformation fed the hopes of the prospective adoptive parents that the child they were procuring wouldn't be a bad investment. If the child had issues, then the birthparents' mysterious DNA could be blamed. If not, then it was all about nurture, never nature.

In the era when I surrendered my son for adoption, newborns were plentiful. White babies of good religious stock, European heritage, preferably untouched by suspicious bloodlines or addiction, were most desirable. The most "worthy" unwed mothers were white, high-achieving college students. The unknown and unasked for details that would have illuminated my family history remained unasked. I was white and invited to live with a wealthy doctor's family, and that said it all.

Who knew the importance of family history and genetics, and who would have told the truth even if the unpleasant realities could be named? I had no idea, at age eighteen, of the prevalence of alcoholism, suicide, and paranoid schizophrenia that lurked in my family tree, not unlike what poet Linda Pastan writes in *In the Old Guerilla War*:

> *The family tree shades us, the snipers waiting in its branches sleep between green leaves.*

I never allowed for the possibility that I wouldn't find my son, but it occurred to me that it might be too late. What if he had died or was dying right now? What if he was a she? What lurked on his birthfather's side of the paternity fence? What if *everything*? In addition to conjuring these obsessive questions, I asked myself the obvious one, *What if he doesn't want to meet me*? I also pondered *What if he doesn't know he's adopted?* And even, *What if he's dangerous*? While not disregarding these cautionary queries, I believed that my son would be inquisitive and dissatisfied with the unnamed space in his life. Richard Uhrlaubi writes in *Culture, Law and Language: Adversarial Motherhood in Adoption:*

> As children who were transferred from one mother to another, adoptees need words to help navigate what in important respects is a dual reality. She or he is simultaneously: a social problem and a precious gift; a symbol of shame and normative family; a source of grief and joy; a human being and a commodity; the answer to one mother's prayers and an alleged threat to another mother's privacy. . . The adopted have lifelong, but different ties to both mothers, each of whom is real.

Since I'd been raised with an adopted brother, I was already familiar with how adoption felt from the inside. When my young, war-widowed mother remarried, the man who would raise me as his daughter adopted me. I attended their wedding as a four-year-old spectator, and it felt perfectly fine to have a new Daddy to call *Daddy*. Despite my parents' best efforts, I felt separate from my blended family—separate and different as a stepchild often feels, a redheaded one at that—aware of spaces that didn't include me. Was my son feeling the same way wherever he was living his life?

My parents *chose* to adopt a child and this is how our family grew. As my mother and I shared a fascination for my new, four-month-old brother, Mark, she would speculate about his mother. She thought that his beautiful curls and chubby legs indicated that he was a prized baby only to have been given up under dire circumstances. My baby brother was always a mischievous but sweet boy, though his curls straightened, and he moved fast and without caution. Soon, he more closely matched the coloring in our family than I did.

I continued my work with Concerned United Birthparents as my somewhere-out-there-son's eighteenth birthday approached, the age which I felt was appropriate to attempt contact with him. We had now settled in Indianapolis, as my husband navigated his strategic corporate climb. Although I had worked fiercely for reform in adoption laws and the availability of records, Kansas was still a closed door in terms of information. I realized that I would need assistance with my quest, so I began looking up private investigators in the Yellow Pages. I called only one number from a pay phone between classes at Butler University, where I was making a second attempt to finish my undergraduate degree in Journalism. During the brief conversation, I made an appointment.

The following day, I arrived at a storefront office which was the antithesis of my ordered life—hectic and high energy, presided over by a ruddy, boisterous, outrageous, way off the grid in bad behavior and big heartedness, Boston-Irish guy. Chuck Keenan was a former FBI agent, now private investigator, and I quickly realized that he was a man I could count on, but someone who should not be crossed. Keenan would return loyalty with loyalty, but only after it was earned. He worked for money, and I was willing to pay any amount for his help.

I told Keenan the story of how I had been forced to surrender my son, now a seasoned, unemotional tale of determination and certainty. He was a worst-case realist, but not without a sense of adventure. I knew I'd found someone who got *it* whatever *it* was—he was a fellow, devoutly-lapsed, cradle Catholic and I knew he might judge me harshly for the intrusion into my son's life. Instead, he seemed more interested in the challenge than in judgment. He warned me that this kind of investigation wouldn't be cheap or easy, "Just like you in high school," he teased at the end of our first meeting. After a dose of Keenan's humor and determination, I was in.

When Keenan agreed to take the case, I suggested that we collaborate. I didn't want to relinquish the search or the process because I wanted to experience the *feelings* which finding my son would bring up—good, bad, ugly. I wanted in on the whole deal with no more mysteries, no more secrets, no more deception and denial. My long-sublimated feelings about this seminal event in my life needed to be realized. I also needed to save money. When I told Keenan how I wanted to work with him to find my son, he said that I had a lot to learn. I persisted, "You can teach me what I need to know." He agreed to a trial partnership, and he then hired me for $10 an hour to be his apprentice investigator on other cases.

He asked me, to my amusement, if I were *tough enough*. I replied, "If walking through hell while nine months pregnant and living to tell about it counts, and if falling from grace in Catholic high school counts, then I'm tough enough." I thought that his question about my fitness had been cheeky, and I knew my job was to educate him about birthmothers, and what we endured giving away our children to a system that judged and exploited us at will. If I wasn't tough enough when I got pregnant in 1963, I became tough enough after I gave birth to my son that night in Kansas. I became tougher each year on my son's birthday. I became tougher when I had my first daughter, but could never tell her that she wasn't actually my first child. I became tougher when I saw redheaded boys who were my son's age, and when I noticed that all Norman Rockwell paintings were of my lost son. The toughening of my heart led to delusion and fantasies that both comforted and confounded.

I was tough enough to withstand opening the padlocked door to my past, to submitting myself to the consequences of breaking a promise I had made to never look back and to never seek my son. I told Keenan that I hoped *he* was tough enough and that I suspected he had a soft heart. I was right on both counts.

My toughness was mostly tenacity. As I earned his respect, Keenan honed my deductive skills and my fortitude for refusals and betrayal, lies and deceptions, and for frequent disparaging, disregard, and disrespect. My part time job as a licensed private investigator included heady assignments from surveillances of wandering spouses to corporate espionage. Once, I wore my fur coat into a posh fur store, asked to see the owner about some alterations, and served him with a subpoena. While some of the assignments were boring and predictable, like watching cheaters do their thing, this job was teaching me more about people than the graduate degrees I would earn in social work and psychology.

Although I could only imagine the ripples I would create as I plowed through bureaucracy and rigid thinking, Keenan knew that I would face daunting resistance and possible failure as I searched for my son. He warned me that I would be fighting my way up the down staircase, that I was embarking on a battle with a drowsy and unpredictable dragon—the state of Kansas adoption system. He cautioned that I could be seriously maligned in my efforts—maybe even jailed—for intruding upon my son's well-meaning, adoptive family.

"Unless they're assholes or in jail themselves," Keenan crowed, "then you win by default. But what if your kid's a criminal or a nut job, who sees that you're rich enough to hire me?" His colorful commentary would accompany me on my quest into the past.

As part of our initial plan, we agreed that Keenan would go to Kansas City to check out the hospital where I'd given birth, and he would also visit the Bureau of Vital Statistics office to see how *closed* certain files were—they were *very closed*, exactly as we had expected. My job, while Keenan traveled on my behalf, was to write to the doctor who had delivered my son, and in whose home I'd lived those five months.

His response was swift, handwritten on his personalized doctor stationery, and resoundingly paternal but not overtly helpful:

> I think you lived with this from the beginning and you have not successfully suppressed it, as you should have. Any wrong you may have done (the onset, not the pregnancy) was more than adequately resolved by your action of giving your child a good home.
>
> Fire burns and you may be playing with fire. You may only want to shed a little light on the matter, as you profess, but you may burn down a

whole life of building for yourself and those about you, past, present and future.

To supply you with too much information could only allow you to enter a dream world. You should have severed the past feelings long ago. No answers are better than any answers that will, whether you know it or not, make your life more miserable, as it might the lives of many other people.

The doctor's response, though well-intentioned, was based on everything he believed and counted on in his experience of matching babies with new parents. Even though his method was ill-conceived, it was part of what maintained a thriving baby market for so long. However, the world of adoption was beginning to change as birthmothers, like me, were reframing those attitudes one woman at a time, and this reframing included a few birthfathers, too. We were mobilized, and we recognized old thinking and shaming when we read it.

No answers were answers in this case. I had discovered a new way of extracting truth even with the doctor's overt denial of information. Keenan was quick to notice certain details in the letter— in *not* telling me what I wanted to know *(Who is my son? How can I find him?)*, the doctor had included other helpful information at no extra charge. All I had to do was interpret the non-responses.

He was raised Catholic, the doctor had written in one portion of the letter (breadcrumbs), *and we see him with his family at mass.*

Catholics most often attended mass in their neighborhood parish. Everyone adhered to those diocesan boundaries, which created community and fellowship. Amidst all this non-information, I figured out where his family attended church—I'd attended mass at this same parish nearly every day when I lived with the doctor's family.

The doctor's refusal to answer my questions ended up being very informative. My son lived! He thrived even! He was part of a good family and he was still in the neighborhood, exactly where I left him. I assumed he went to the local Catholic school and how many redheaded boys could there be in his class?

Whenever I sought something or someone I had lost, I said my prayer to Saint Anthony, "Tony, Tony, come around. Something's lost and can't be found." My luck with that plea was testimony to Saint Anthony's skill in finding things.

Keenan was jubilant with the doctor's letter, since the hospital and the Kansas Bureau of Vital Statistics said *no* to granting us any information, and they meant it. What he did turn up in Kansas, however, was the name of the attorney of record on the adoption papers. Keenan sent me home to write another letter—this particular one was to be written with feigned innocence. I asked the attorney from the adoption proceeding what I considered a simple request—if my son's adoptive parents would be willing to receive additional information about me. To which I added that I would like to meet *their* son, under supervision.

My son was now a year short of his eighteenth birthday—the time when I felt comfortable approaching him directly. I decided that I would never ask again if this letter failed. We still had no idea who his adoptive parents were, but we had the first thread to follow. Keenan and I recognized the clues which were provided by an unwitting doctor telling us *no* very firmly.

I was a strong enough writer to impress and impact the reader with my sincere sorrow about surrendering my son, along with my *need to know* and *to be known*. I meant it. I refused to be part of the conspiracy that labeled me and distanced me from grief or information.

The same reasoning applied to my son, who was being denied knowledge of the one person who actually looked like him and shared his heritage. I failed to see how my appearance in his life, if handled consciously, would do anything but provide more love and possibility. It was then that I knew the infinite capacity of love, not only of a mother for a son, but *this* son could be loved by more than one mother. I was realistic about the role of his adoptive family—reuniting with my son was not to spite them, but to empower *him*.

While the attorney's response to my letter was sympathetic and kind, it held no hope for a mother and child reunion:

> The adoptive parents are clients of long-standing with this firm. They are Catholic and of high moral integrity. Further, they are middle-class people who have a good home environment. I shall contact them and if they desire that their adopted son determine your name and address, I shall inform you accordingly.

My son's adoptive parents were protective and

territorial. I worried that I could never convince his adoptive mother that I was anything but a threat. I had been told to expect this reaction from the adoptive family, though I took it as a sign that no door was truly closed; we just needed to pick the right lock. Maybe I should have tried my little, red luggage key.

My next step was to write a considered letter, using a template suggested by CUB, to a district court judge, who was the best person to receive my request for access to records. In part, I wrote:

> In order that court records be updated to reflect my intentions and wishes regarding my birthchild, and in anticipation of a legislative change which may make my birthchild's access to my identity contingent upon my permission, I should like to grant the court my express permission to release identifying information to my birthchild upon his request.

Adopted children in Kansas had the right to their adoption records, which were closed only to the birthmother. I wanted to cover that contingency. If my son was looking for me, I didn't want us to be working at cross-purposes. This buried information defined obsolete thinking based on the idea of reparation (mine) and a presumed need for protection from something unknown and untested (his).

I was referred to a different court and had to petition another judge. I asked only that my information be placed in my son's file along with a copy of the consent form I had signed at the time of the adoption. In my ongoing quest to collect breadcrumbs, this would be a prize that could not be denied once a judge was found who would agree to grant my request. My research proved that everything I had asked for in terms of information and records was within the parameters of the law. It remained up to the discretion of this judge.

Months later I received a reply, and the judge *apologized* to *me*:

> First, I apologize for the delay in answering your fine letter, occasioned by the press of other Court business. Also, upon reading your letter I was immediately aware that the depth and seriousness of the matters presented would require considerable thought and deliberate study on our part.

This *fine* letter I'd spent nearly eighteen years drafting and living, was written in truth, just as I'd written to the doctor, the lawyer, the case workers, hospitals, legislators, and countless others. She believed me and wasn't judging me for wanting to go up the down staircase. Along with her belief in my good intentions, she would provide the ultimate empowerment:

> I would like you to know that in the seven years I have served as Judge of the Court handling all adoptions in this County, I have never received a more intelligently and sensitively written inquiry in this area. There is nothing you have stated in your letter, with which we are not in complete sympathy, and are most willing to utilize the good offices of this District Court to assist you in accomplishing your stated goals. Finally, I would

commend you for the fact that your views and position are based upon a great regard for the rights and feelings of all persons involved. This factor is the primary one in motivating us to ultimate efforts on your behalf.

In addition, this judge wrote to the court that I had previously petitioned:

It would seem that what this birthmother needs and wants is a copy of the Consent form she signed with the reference to the adoptive parents expunged. I realize this request falls into a very novel and unprecedented area but couldn't this request be viewed as falling within the contemplation of KSA992278?

It was through my membership in CUB that I learned of the vital importance of certain documents contained in those elusive adoption files. Some of the information was actually mine by law, since I had signed the papers and had never received copies of what I had signed.

Expunging names wasn't going to keep me from seeing the number attached to the document, and with that, the house of cards built to protect a punitive system, would fall, revealing the rooms within. My intention to meet my son was clear and purposeful. By this time, I had other plans in the works. Chuck Keenan, now my trusted friend, was helpful in discerning the valuable information from the crap information. He considered the judge's letter a jewel.

After the benevolence of this judge, I simply sent

a check for $3.00 to the first judge whom I had written. He would include my check with a letter to the clerk, who would open the sealed adoption records and provide me the original birth certificate I had signed the day I surrendered my son for adoption.

Why would I want a document that would tell me nothing more than what I already knew? I had now learned from other correspondence that there was *always* something to be discovered. If nothing else, I would know *with certainty* that I had given birth to a son on the very date I had been instructed to forget. No one accounted for my pitch-perfect memory and for my ability to recall fine details, even under pressure. No one insisted I take this journey of discovery, but I had to. I had been forbidden to see my son when he was born, to name him, to know if he lived or died. I had been reassured that he was indeed a perfect child for someone else. My parting gift along with false assurances, was a map written in reappearing ink.

With each success, defeat, refused access, and with each dead end, Keenan and I rejoiced. Sometimes we fumed at the system, which tried to deter us, but we remained relentless and optimistic.

I waited a few weeks for the original birth certificate to arrive in the mail. It was a simple, photocopied document with my name on the *mother's name* line. The baby line read *Baby* with my maiden name, which was an improvement upon *Bastard,* a designation used in prior decades. The father was identified as *information withheld*. Another convenient deception, since I had never willingly withheld the identity of my son's birthfather. Had the system been protecting him, too? The injustice stunned me.   As I learned subsequently, *information withheld* stands forever as the definitive information on my son's original birth certificate.

As non-disclosing as this document was intended to be, it gave me the ability to know my son's identity based on the information I had already gathered. In order to change the birth certificate to reflect his birthfather's name, our son must rescind his adoption. This varied from state to state, and Kansas seemed to remain in the dark ages.

Keenan and I created a list of the boys graduating from the Catholic high schools located near the doctor's neighborhood. The photos we obtained were in color, which was crucial since we were looking for a boy with red hair. We narrowed it down to a small graduating class. If we had figured the math correctly, if the stars were in alignment, and if he hadn't skipped or failed a grade along the way, he was one of three possible boys.

Evelyn, a Kansas City birthmother, chimney sweep, and CUB member, offered to attend the upcoming graduation on my behalf. She would take photos of the three likely boys whom I had identified, then she would mail the photos to me so that I could judge whether one of them was indeed my son. Since this was the early 1980s, there was no instant way to send photos. I was on edge the night of graduation, but in a hopeful way.

This targeted graduation was held in the church where I had attended mass. The irony wasn't lost on me. I had prayed there many times for deliverance from the hell I was living, and I had asked for reinstatement as a *good girl.* True to her word, Evelyn attended the graduation, took photos of the likely candidates, and as a birthmother herself, noticed all of the important things. She had yet to begin her search for her own daughter, but she was a wonderful stand-in for me.

It took over a week for the pictures to arrive, even though she had sent them airmail, an extravagance for which I repaid her $5.00 in postage and fees. Awaiting the mail was not easy, considering the expectations I held for those photos. I envisioned them lost en route, confiscated by the birthmother police, burned in a mail truck fire, or faded to white due to a fatal processing error in the darkroom.

I was maintaining my vigil for the mail when a long white envelope was dropped through the door slot. It landed on the entry floor with a satisfied swoop, and I watched it glide to a stop. There was no mystery that this was the envelope full of pictures—my x-ray vision was in place, and I could read the return address from Kansas City. I picked it up, and ripped it open where I stood.

The photos, only a scant few, were all of one red-haired boy in a blue-tasseled mortarboard who looked very serious, intent upon the ceremony, and slightly nervous. He looked familiar, and he looked fantastic in blue. I scanned the grainy pictures for characteristics that could belong to me or to Joe. This boy seemed to be the perfect combination of his birthparents' faces. As I looked carefully, I believed that I was seeing my son for the first time.

Evelyn knew who his family was because of the cheering and applauding when his name was called as he received his diploma. She had also observed this redheaded student hugging these same people after the ceremony, and she noticed how sweetly he interacted with the woman she assumed was his grandmother. There was no doubt to me that he was adopted—he looked nothing like them. His adoptive parents were older than me by a decade. The rest of the family group included the proud grandmother and three brothers, who looked as much like his adoptive parents as he did not. I had made the right choice not to attend the graduation, as the resemblance between this redheaded boy and I might have seriously distracted from the occasion.

Along with the photos, something else slipped out—Evelyn had included the graduation program. As I unfolded it, I immediately noticed that she had starred one particular boy's last name and had added some excited exclamation marks. With this new information, I could obtain a copy of his amended birth certificate from the Bureau of Vital Statistics. Closed records be damned. I was doing what any mother lion would do to get her cub back into the pride. Keenan had been training me well.

I requested the amended birth certificate and it arrived in less time than the surreptitious photos, and I hadn't paid for airmail. The Bureau of Vital Statistics needed only a money order and my wish would be granted. The letter arrived a few days later, and I laid it next to the original birth certificate on my little desk in the converted laundry room. All of the information matched: the number on the top of both certificates, the birth date and time, length and weight of baby (all news to me, as I had never been given an opportunity to see this information). Check, check, check, check. Could it be?

As I read through the documents at my desk, I knew that I had found my son. I was certain—my maiden name and the *information withheld* birthfather's name had been replaced by the names of the adoptive parents.

Not to put too fine a point on serendipity or to

my connection with the saints, but I had secretly named my son Andrew Joseph just after he was born. His birthday was on the feast of the little-known, but miracle-working St. Andrew of Corsini. Coincidence, sign, or breadcrumb—his middle name on the amended birth certificate was Andrew.

Keenan was again ecstatic with all of this new information, and then he asked me the question which identically matched my husband's concern, "Now what?"

In the spirit of providing information, I wrote another letter, this time to my son. I needed to explain why and what I'd done to find him, providing him a capsule version of my life, describing his three siblings, and telling him how he could reach me. Though I knew where he lived, I hesitated to send the letter to his parents' home. I rightfully feared that he would never see it and that their lawyer would become my new pen pal. I decided to hang on to this letter, and I ended up constantly revising it.

Though writing letters was cathartic for me, I was becoming impatient and beyond curious. I felt strongly that I should go to Kansas City and give it to him myself.

There were few gray areas left to explore, except for the biggest mystery of all—would this boy want to meet the woman who had other children only a few years after his birth? Would he be angry, insulted, murderous, damaged by my actions? Would he find all of this untenable and threatening? Was it too late for me to consider these things?

Keenan was distracted by a major case, and he assumed that I would be temporarily satisfied with having found *the kid,* as he called him. I kept my amended plan about traveling to Kansas City to myself. I didn't want Keenan to attempt to stop me from doing the one thing that lingered in my mind. My plan was potentially bad for this young man about to go to college, bad for his parents who might be litigious, bad for my family and for my marriage, yet I persisted.

I was fervent about reversing time and destiny and I had become singularly focused on seeing this to the end, whatever *this* might mean. I was on a mission and it was not yet completed. Without the blessing of the trusted people in my life, I took one, last step toward finality and closure. A letter from my father granted me passage:

> My Dear,
>
> I love you too much to try and imply approval or disapproval of what you are doing. We, your mother and I, influenced you in the initial action because of your age and the times. Now you are an adult and no longer in my protective care, and if some psychological need requires you to locate your son, then I am all for it. Not for the good of my grandson, but because my daughter needs this to round out her need to be a whole, mature person. Maturity according to Webster is, "to bring or come to full development," but it is also, "payable or due." So, one might preclude that the note is payable and due and it is time for you to collect a long, overdue bill. The account can be marked closed.
>
> Know that you are now going through another trauma and I hope you forgive your

mother and I for our actions, which at the time were appropriate. I guess what I am trying to say is that I do approve of your action. I'm here for you if you need help.

All my love,
Dad

This letter demonstrated to me how an adopted daughter *is* a daughter in every sense, and how an adopted father only enhances her life, while guiding her toward her heart's desire.

VIII

Gray Market

Kansas City

1982

There was no doubt that I was heading back to Kansas to face down my past and that sleeping dragon. It had been eighteen years since I had last been in Kansas City, and I was thirty-six and no longer the girl who had blindly abdicated the power to make her own decisions. The dragon guarding the gates of the Kansas adoption system insisted upon the continued separation of mother from child. It was the gray area of legality, of moral judgment by the same coda that had held me in its grip for nearly two decades, along with countless women in my same circumstance.

This "gray market" adoption, which I had unwillingly participated in, was executed outside the adoption agency. It involved private attorneys keeping evidence in locked files and surrender papers signed at kitchen tables. I was now determined to render everything that was murky gray into clear black and white. I considered it my job as this young man's birthmother to offer him the truth—no more secrets encoded with embellished facts.

Packing a few family pictures, the unsent letter to my son, and my unnamed fears into an old red suitcase, I embarked on a road trip to Kansas from Indiana. I would be returning to the exact location where I had left my son, with only a vague notion of what I would do upon my arrival.

Before setting out on my trip, I had enlisted the support and the good company of a willing conspiratorial girlfriend, aptly named Mary Smith. Our rudimentary plan involved Mary calling my unsuspecting son and telling him that she was a reporter for the local paper. This local paper would be working on an article about recent high school graduates. Not a terribly original cover story, but I had learned to always *KISS—Keep it Simple, Stupid,* which makes deception easier to manage under pressure.

Mary called the home of my son's adoptive parents and calmly asked for him when his mother answered the phone. She gave him the story about the newspaper article, and then she named a park near his house as the ideal meeting place for the interview. Mary and I had concocted the idea for this faux interview in the park, as we spent a few hours of reconnaissance in his neighborhood, considering what would feel both safe and familiar to him.

Mary was as fearless as I was terrified. We had discussed the possibility that my son might not be interested in meeting with a newspaper reporter, no matter how flattering the premise, and that my trip to Kansas would yield nothing. Perhaps my son hadn't inherited my personality traits at all, but had a more shy or fearful temperament. I did believe, however, on some recently discovered maternal level, that he would agree to the meeting and interview without hesitation. I shared the phone receiver with Mary as she spoke with him—I heard my son's young smiling voice for the first time. It held an innocent cadence and a sweetness I hoped our meeting wouldn't change.

Mary and I had checked into a motel about six blocks from the doctor's house, which bridged the gap between where I'd lived in exile eighteen years ago and where my son lived now. It was only a few walkable blocks between the past and present. He had always been exactly where I left him. My greatest fear wasn't blowing open the full-metal, fail-safe vault door, but being seen by the doctor or his wife as I surveyed the neighborhood. My son had the right to decide for himself whether or not he wanted to know me. I even considered the possibility of a run-in with the *unwed mother police*, determined to arrest me for trespassing in my surrendered son's life.

Our first surreptitious evening in Kansas City passed without incident. I talked to Mary about my memories of living here in 1964—walking to church, the cemetery outside my bedroom window, the trips to the record store in Prairie Village, and my two Barbra Streisand albums, played constantly until they were as thin as holy wafers. I was now far different, yet I was exactly this same young woman, and I had come back to right all wrongs.

On the day of the "interview," our plan was to wait for my son in the parking area of the park where the meeting would take place. He had told Mary that he would be at a picnic table near the field where he played on a baseball team. We drove into the lot just as my son was getting out of his mother's car—the possibility that one of his parents would drop him off had never occurred to me. Immediately, I slid to the floor of the passenger seat, fearful that his adoptive mother might be suspicious of a redheaded woman in a car with Indiana license plates, who happened to closely resemble her son. Mary planned to remain in the car until she was sure that my son would talk to me. Then, she would walk to a phone booth and call a cab to take her back to the hotel.

Once his mother drove away, I watched my son— a shiny vision of a tall and tan young man, dressed in white tennis shorts and shirt, walking purposefully toward a new reality. He seemed disembodied and ethereal. I connected the actual presence of this redheaded person with the envisioned baby of my fantasy, and it flowed from a place I had long ago considered inaccessible. He was beautiful and familiar and oblivious to how his life would suddenly change in a few minutes, as I walked toward him.

I forced myself to stay in the present and to indelibly imprint in my memory that moment of seeing him. He was part of me. He existed because of me. We had, for nine months, shared life. I recognized a stirring, maternal love on both a new and familiar level of fierceness.

As he walked down the incline toward the picnic area, it was as if eighteen years became inconsequential. I noticed the small grocery store across from the park. This store had been one of my approved excursion destinations when I had lived with the doctor's family. I remembered its ripe comingled smells of meat, fresh doughnuts, and wood polish; its few aisles of food and paper goods culminating in two checkout stands; a meat counter at the very back where I picked up the steaks the doctor's wife ordered in advance; a tiered magazine rack with current issues of *Teen, Seventeen*, and *Mademoiselle*; and a candy counter where I bought red licorice. I assumed that everyone who worked there knew I was the latest girl to live with the doctor's family. The household shopping list had always included two cartons of cigarettes for the doctor and his wife. Fortunately, I was forbidden to smoke (though I did steal a cigarette from the doctor occasionally). In 1963, there was no medical sanction on smoking while pregnant. Back then, I was forbidden access to many things, but on this day here in Kansas City, I was kicking open the door.

I walked down the little hill toward my son's curious face. Mary watched our historic reunion from her car, telling me later that we were perfectly matched, and that she had been part of something magical and a little dangerous.

At first, it was like seeing a new version of Joe at the age when I had last seen him—the night I left for college. Then, I saw my ancestors and myself in him, as he merged into a wholly new and astonishing person. I was witnessing a collision of DNA, youth, hope, and innocent trust. In exchange, I offered a woman whom he couldn't possibly mistake for anyone but his coincidental twin. I had practiced saying, "Hello, I am your other mother," but he spoke first:

"I know who you are."

"I am your *other* mother."

He laughed and said, "I thought you were Sue Ellen on *Dallas*."

He looked amused and tried to pretend he wasn't surprised. His nervousness was camouflaged by a barrage of questions, which I willingly answered as fast as he asked.

"Who is my father?"

I figured that I had a slim chance of redemption in this kid's eyes if I committed, without reservation, to introduce him to his birthfather.

"I know who he is, and I'll make sure you meet him."

Though I didn't know much about Joe's present status, our son's need to know about his birthfather seemed paramount. It was, after all, the first question he asked me. I vowed right then to bring them together.

As we began to talk, he shared with me that at fourteen years old, he'd missed having a man with whom he could speak frankly about his approaching adulthood. Perhaps it was an unnamed yearning for his birthfather.

Although he lived with a loving family, open discussions weren't common.

That day, my son wanted me to know, as do many adoptees, that he had a great life with good parents whom he loved, three brothers who were not adopted, a special grandmother, lots of cousins, a car he could drive, a love of baseball, and no girlfriend, but lots of girls who were his friends.

"So," he eventually asked, "did you consider having an abortion when you found out you were pregnant with me?"

I told him the condensed version of the story— what few choices I had, and how society, *our* church, and my parents made my decisions for me. Abortion wasn't among them, neither was marriage or parenting on my own. Adoption was the *best* choice and I had believed it was perfect for him. It was too soon to fill in the spaces that so closely held my pain and loss.

He wanted to hear about my parents and his other relatives. I told him about those who preceded him, those he would meet, and those he had missed. On this July morning in my son's neighborhood park, he claimed his place among the branches of our family tree.

"You're Irish," I told him. "Big time Irish, and you come from a long line of redheads."

"Then, I'll probably have redheaded kids, right?" he prophesized.

As I answered his questions for several hours, we discovered how easy it was for us to talk. He told me that there were snowflakes the size of silver dollars falling on the day his parents first brought him home. At age five, he had been told that he was adopted after asking his mother why he had red hair, but no one else in the family did. He loved it when he discovered that he tanned better than me, that he had more freckles, and that I had gone to all of this trouble to find him. He would be going to the University of Kansas in the fall and, yes, I could buy him lunch today. He chose the A & W, where we continued to talk over papa and mama burgers with fries and Coke.

As we drove back to his parents' house, I pretended that I had no idea where he lived, letting him give me directions. I did not want him to know how much I already knew about his life, or that I had no intention of ever losing him again. I dropped him off at his house with a promise to wait for *him* to be in touch with *me*. I also gave him the handwritten letter I had revised the previous night in the motel. That letter was written in unshed tears and heart blood, sealed with the hopes and dreams of an eighteen-year-old girl mired in the confusion of 1964 and signed by the *birthmother* of 1982. I felt love for my child, but I did not dare tell him yet. This unsuspecting, but familiar boy had enough to consider for one day.

That night, I took Mary, my co-conspirator, with me to meet the fellow birthmother, Evelyn, who had attended my son's graduation and had taken the photos. I owed both of these women a debt I could never repay. We rode in a horse drawn carriage around the Country Club Plaza, the place I had been the day President Kennedy was assassinated, the other seismic event in 1963. The three of us talked about meeting my son, which was still an anomaly for birthparents in those days, even considered dangerous. We spoke about Evelyn's hoped for, but yet unrealized, reunion with her daughter. The laborious search for and discovery of my son had become a flat fact since that morning. The drama of the search, the discoveries, the frustrations, and sorrows were now reduced to this: *I had a son, whom I gave up for adoption, and I found him today.*

Mary and Evelyn were the first people to witness my new reality. Though I was probably in some degree of shock because of the day's events, I felt like a woman in love. I once heard a birthmother describe her relationship with her newly found son as *feeling like a love affair.* I could relate—I was smitten with him, sharing every detail about him in a continual loop, hoping he would call soon, and voicing my plans for the relationship I envisioned with him.

Back at the motel, I called home to tell my husband that I'd met my son. He responded in a passive aggressive way, obviously fearful of what might happen next, "The phone bill came today and it's over $100. Is this about finished now?"

As a woman newly "in love," I was stunned by my husband's reaction to my joyous news. I knew that nothing was finished, and in fact, some things were just beginning. This response, however, I kept to myself.

Having told my complete story to Mary and Evelyn, I found myself recalling the Irish myth about a storyteller who would share the history of Ireland at the hearth fire of strangers in exchange for sanctuary and a place to rest. Recounting my lived experience of becoming pregnant in 1963, then surrendering my baby for adoption had become mythical. I would tell it and retell it to surprised, empathic, judgmental, and disapproving audiences. I would tell my story without fear of recrimination because what could I lose now that would rival the loss of my first-born child?

In the early 1980s, I searched for and found my son—doing whatever I had to do—for myself and for my surrendered child. Other birthmothers did the same. Our goal was to square the tilted and inequitable past, changing the practice of blaming the victim. We wanted the world to know that punishing birthmothers might not be the most productive response. As numerous birthparents emerged, my actions were more justified. And united, we were a daunting group.

I left Kansas City, returned to Indiana, and immediately began searching for my son's birthfather, Joe. It was time for him to know the truth, even though this would impact the "idyllic life" that I assumed he led. He needed to be informed that *he* was next up for a surprise meeting. I figured that if I were walking out of a closet, I would bring him out with me. I suspected he'd never mentioned his first child to anyone. Not that I knew with certainty, but I had learned not to second-guess the past.

I expected some predictable reactions from him: a disclaimer and rejection; denial, perhaps grounded in his mother's ancient threat to name other potential birthfathers; or, more romantically, a braver response that would validate the months we spent together after I returned home from Kansas. I considered those days before I left for college—forged with unspoken grief and a Lindy star sapphire ring.

Computers with search engines were years from development. I had to find Joe by working in reverse through phonebooks, public records, city directories, and calling research librarians. I had learned from the investigative world and my time with Chuck Keenan, to start with what I already knew. I phoned Joe's mother, pretending to be one of her son's high school friends (not a former girlfriend), and she provided a bounty of information. Generous and unthreatened, she told me where he lived and worked.

I came to my search for Joe with information that was twenty years old. After our emotional parting when I took the train to Denver, I came home that Christmas certain we would see each other. I started making calls from the beige wall phone with the twisty cord in my mother's kitchen. Two phone calls into my inquiry, I learned he was getting married. Apparently, the next girl who became pregnant *was* marriage material. Or, as the romantic side of me believed, he did not want to lose a second child. My mother later told me that his wife had given birth to a stillborn baby boy. Joe's mother had called her after it happened to inquire about my son, to which my mother replied with her Irish completely up, "What baby?"

My son's birthfather had lost two sons by the time he was nineteen. He stayed married to his wife for sixteen years, leaving her for his secretary.

There was a part of me savoring the possibility of a long, overdue acknowledgement that we had a son and that he would subsequently be forced to tell his family. There was another part of me that knew, however, that I could be rejected by Joe, along with our son. I had no urge to ruin Joe's life—I wanted my son to know that his father's name was no longer *withheld*. I was amending my son's amended birth certificate one line at a time, filling in the blanks, correcting the lies, lifting the secrecy, and the order of protection.

When I took my independent investigation and discovery to Chuck Keenan, which included a full account of meeting my son in the park, I expected a lecture about messing with people's lives. Instead, I earned his enthusiastic agreement to contact my son's birthfather for me. He also asked me if *enough would ever be enough*. My answer, "No, is it ever?" surprised neither of us.

By then, we had evolved from client to coworker, into genuine friendship. I felt like a fixture in his life and he was certainly one in mine. We visited each other's houses and were acquainted with one another's kids and spouses well enough for his wife to frequently tell us that we were both nuts.

He had a riotous home in one of the historic suburbs of Indianapolis, full of energy, laughter, and something always cooking in a big pot on the stove. He had all sons and one daughter, the youngest, who was his baby girl. He was a classic tough guy with a heart of gold—maybe copper along with his sins. I was working with him on other cases as his girl sidekick. We had involved ourselves in all manner of secret surveillance and false pretense. We shared secrets and grudges.

Keenan was my most trusted friend and mentor, and his singular involvement in finding my son was an education about life tempered with tenacity. His wife said that we deserved each other. Becoming the older brother I never had, Keenan treated me with the loving disrespect of a sibling. He gave me a more powerful voice, validating my need to know the truth, admiring my work, but scolding me when I made stupid mistakes with an investigation—failing to notice important details or otherwise costing him money.

That afternoon in his office, Keenan picked up the

phone and called my son's birthfather. I held my breath as he assumed his best imitation of a concerned detached detective, "Hi, Joe. I'm a private investigator in Indianapolis. My client is looking for you because you two had a baby together in 1964. Do you know what I'm talking about, Sir?"

Holy shit. He was actually talking to Joe. Keenan adlibbed his way through a conversation I could only half comprehend—not because I was only hearing one side of it. My past was colliding with the present in a cluttered office and not in a positive way. I thought, *What if Joe doesn't remember me?* I was suddenly overwhelmed with second guesses and insecurities. I even dredged up, *Maybe the doctor was correct, telling me that I had no right to look behind the wall people built for me nearly twenty years ago.*

Therein, lurked my shame, my secret, my son, and my first love, who had abandoned me without a backward glance. So what if he was seventeen and still a junior in high school. He was old enough to have sex with me, and hadn't we been in love?

"There you go," Keenan crowed as hung up the phone, "Daddy wants to meet the kid, but first he wants to talk to you. Maybe that's what you wanted, but you need to be very careful with this guy. This isn't like meeting some eighteen-year-old kid, you know. You could actually get hurt all over again."

Keenan's blatant opinion wasn't lost on me; I just couldn't hear him. When had I ever listened to anyone when it came to Joe? Maybe *this time* I was collecting a karmic debt, that long-overdue note my father had mentioned in his letter. This was a risk I was willing to take—I had made our son a promise in a park about meeting his birthfather.

There was only silence from the University of Kansas during the first months of my son's freshman year. When he finally called me, wanting to get together again, I had been forging a flirty phone relationship with his birthfather. I was imperviously heading toward *that* predicted disaster, but I was doing it with fierce determination and justification. I was going to introduce my son to his father, and I was the one with the secret.

One of my favorite payback fantasies unfolded like this: Joe would see me and I would be so fabulous, gorgeous, and brilliant that he would find me irresistible. In return, I would feel nothing. I would be strong and emboldened by the success of my search and claiming our son. I hoped my instincts were as right about him as they had been about our son. It was a gamble because he might not be interested in either of us.

IX

White Out

Kansas City

1982

I believed that introducing a young man to his father for the first time could create a shift in the earth's rotation, cause cosmic collisions, and induce the collective cringe of Kansas lawmakers who write and enforce archaic adoption laws.

Keenan drove me to the airport in Indianapolis the day that I would be flying to meet Joe in Kansas City. Uncharacteristically emotional, Keenan kissed me on the forehead as I got out of the car and said, "I'm worried about you, kid, but not for the first time. Be careful of old boyfriends, promise?"

As I exited the airplane in Kansas City, Joe was standing in the terminal waiting for me. His eyes were the same as when we were teenagers, but I had to search for the face I remembered. Joe had aged and it surprised me. Seeing his sexy spirit, which had once captivated me, took some imagining on my part. Beneath the travails of time and too much corporate booze, I recognized him as both changed and unchanged. I wasn't sure if my initial impression of this older Joe was a good thing. Keenan's warning about "old boyfriends" became a cautionary song playing in my mind as Joe and I hugged for the first time in two decades.

As planned, we drove together to the University of Kansas in Lawrence to see *our* son. Joe would be meeting him for the first time, and I would be reconnecting with him a second time. The drive between Kansas City and Lawrence was through a blinding snowstorm, but I knew Keenan had been alluding to *other* dangers when he kissed my forehead.

The snow made me a nervous passenger, but I felt safe with Joe, who navigated better than I could, although the highway was nearly closed to traffic. Since many significant events in our former relationship had happened in his car—planning our future together, lovemaking, arguing—it was familiar territory. I quickly assumed the passenger position, with no urge to slide over and drape myself around him. Leading up to these travel plans, we had caught up with each other's lives through phone calls, talking about my search for our son, recapturing the years in between, and putting to rest many of the fears and myths, which we had carried about each other in the interim.

Each of us claimed happy marriages—his was newer than mine, after recently divorcing the woman with whom he had raised his family. I couldn't understand why they had remained married for almost two decades, raising three children, burying one tiny stillborn, only to end it with acrimony and resentment. His story included an overlapping relationship with his secretary. Joe said that his wife resisted losing him, and I related to her across time.

I asked him why he married *her* instead of *me*, as though I was still firmly tethered to our past. His answer was simple, "I didn't want to go through that again."

I immediately thought, *Go through what? I went through everything for you.*

I realized that my feelings were not entirely about *him*, but were about *me* wishing I could redo our relationship, and in addition, keep my current kids, my husband, and my complete life. My agenda was less clear and more confused by the fiery collision of our unfinished past with our reconfigured present. Stephen King's *Pet Cemetery* came to mind as we drove—the place where all dead things return, but not exactly in their original form. In fact, they were often quite rotten.

I don't believe that either of us disclosed the full truth about our marriages. While my husband knew that I was going to Kansas to visit my son, I hadn't told him it was for an additional reunion with my son's father. Happily married people don't arrange meetings in Kansas snowstorms, no matter how well intentioned, without a hidden agenda. I didn't fully understand Joe's motivation for our rendezvous, since he was newly remarried, but I certainly knew my purpose. For a thousand unspoken reasons, I justified my deception, which felt exactly right in order to introduce father to son.

In this second visit with my son, I felt that I had earned this moment. I reflected upon the tangled road that brought me to here and congratulated myself for realizing this comingling of fact and fantasy, which now constituted my reality. I had always envisioned a substantial fantasy-wish about meeting a lost parent. Since my father had been killed in the war when I was only three weeks old, I had never seen, heard, or felt his presence in an earthly way. I, like my son, always knew that my parent was *out there* somewhere.

Unlike my son, my father and I could never meet. Sometimes I would pretend that my father had survived the direct hit to his fighter plane, which had exploded and crashed over East Germany. In my fantasy, he had landed safely, but for some reason, he was unable to contact us. When my mother and adopted father would argue violently, I would pray for my *real* father to appear suddenly so that he could take my mother and me away. I would, in this pretend world, challenge my mother to choose which of her husbands she loved best. Accordingly, she would always choose her young, dead husband—my *real* father. What happened to my remaining siblings was not under any practical consideration in the new reality I was creating. I voted for romance to prevail.

Thus, I imagined that I was somehow contributing to karmic balance by navigating this terrible snowstorm in order to introduce my son to his birthfather, as I had promised. It felt primal and necessary as we navigated in white blindness.

By the time we finally reached Lawrence, the snow had stopped enough for our son to be waiting in the circle-drive outside his dorm. He hugged me in that sideways manner of self-conscious boys, and he grinned as he shook his birthfather's hand.

"This is your birthfather, Joe."

Thus began our family reunion, and I was fully aware of the reality I had so laboriously created from a wish and dream. Our son had chosen to keep our meeting from his adoptive parents, and we were able to sequester ourselves in a what-could-have-been parent and son bubble. Bubbles burst, but ours was strong and clear at this moment.

We decided to eat dinner at a steakhouse, where I witnessed the ritual of men, which always involves taking measure of each other. They talked about Jayhawks, Royals, and Chiefs, family history, Austrian heritage, four more siblings, a grandmother, aunts, uncles, and cousins. They covered all of the essential paternal pieces. Joe had brought a family tree, which he unrolled on the table, dishes pushed aside. His paternal history was rich with information. My son wasn't as Irish as I had predicted, but he happily claimed his newly revealed heritage with fascination and endless questions only Joe could answer.

"Tell me about you two," our inquisitive son later asked, "What did you think when you found out she was pregnant? Did you love her?"

Joe told him how we had met and that we loved each other. We were powerless teenagers, he recounted, in a world organized by our parents. It was a version of the story I had never heard—how Joe wanted to keep our baby, but had no way to make it happen. I was glad to hear Joe say this, even if I suspected his selective memory. His soft and sincere response tempted me to believe that I had not been alone in 1963, though in reality, the consequences were all mine.

I listened carefully and observed father and son with what I recognized as a resurgence of love and something new. There was too much of my battered heart exposed on the table with those slabs of rare steak, which I wasn't able to eat—not now and not when I was pregnant at the doctor's table.

Steak again! I thought, *Why is steak always part of this story?*

The meal was over before I was ready to stop watching them and cataloging their astonishing, matching qualities—their identical hands and mannerisms. Our son's face looked like both of us, further defining our comingled DNA. All of the best qualities of Joe and I were on display in him, and it wouldn't take a paternity or a maternity test to determine that he was ours. While I had no intention of throwing over my existing family of children, there was a part of me that was already inserting my son into the family Christmas photo, if he were willing. I also envisioned a scene where Joe and I had been married for eighteen years, and we were taking *our* son out to dinner. These pictures flickered across my mind, then faded into anger.

After our lengthy dinner conversation, we dropped our son off at his dorm and we headed back to Kansas City. The snow had stopped and the return drive was less stressful, but I found myself consumed with a simmering fury and resentment which were about to become unleashed. This was grief tied up in the worn wrapping of sublimation and the emerging doubt that what I did *was best* for my son. I began to fear that my supposed unselfish act had been a sham. Here was Joe, recently married to a woman for whom he had left his first wife and their children. *Could that have been me?* He now represented even more evidence of what I'd lost—this merged with the pain of having been separated from my son.

The traumatic events that occurred eighteen years ago—how my son's life had been arbitrarily amended, how I'd been required to walk away without seeing or touching him—were, at this moment, a searing reality on a highway in Kansas. Minus the regulatory expectations from society, parents, church, and the state of Kansas— my son's birth had been an experience of devastation, sadness, and singular grief. This grief had waited, unacknowledged, and it had grown exponentially to the level of repression. It was about to explode like the wretched snowstorm of that afternoon—unrelenting, blind, and dangerous.

I barely spoke in the car as we traveled back to Kansas City, afraid that I might scream at this man, whom I barely knew, yet knew too well: *Don't you get it? Don't you see what I did because you left me? That boy is our son. Please feel something and don't normalize the experience so quickly. Stop telling me about the kids you had with your first wife, how perfect they are and how devoted you are to them.*

No psychologist would be surprised to hear that amidst this symbolic snowstorm, my long repressed feelings suddenly erupted. I started to cry, mourning from the vacant space beneath my heart. I wanted Joe to hurt a mere percentage of the grief that I was experiencing— then and *now*. I'd been processing the surrendering of my son for two decades. It had taken me the last few years just to become accustomed to the reversal of fortune I was currently enjoying. This father and son reunion was supposed to be the culmination of my reverse journey, transforming misery to happiness.

Joe pulled off the highway and stopped the car. He held me for a long time until I was finished crying. I said to him, "I hate you. You left me with no choice but to give away that amazing boy you just met."

"I understand how you feel," Joe claimed, trying to console me.

I then let Joe know that I *hated* him for being so cavalier about how great this reunion had been without acknowledging the truth of our loss. If Joe was feeling any sorrow, he didn't show it. I hated that, too. I hated him for acting like meeting our son was some country club event. I hated him for marrying someone else and not me. I hated him so much that I wondered if I still loved him, and where would that get me?

I took a breath in the icy Kansas air. Finally, I was able to say, "I hope my son will be in *my* life from this point forward. You need to know that I'm only responsible for my relationship with him, and whatever happens next between the two of you, is up to *you*. You can be there for him or you can choose not to."

Joe's elation about the reunion with his son, which I arranged and made happen, only fed my anger at him and at the sacrificial altar of societal expectations upon which I had been forced to place our beautiful baby. I saw that Joe was now reaping benefits that he hadn't earned. I, not he, had carried that loss every day for nine months, and subsequently, for eighteen years. He had, to my knowledge, never looked back after our last meeting in 1964, the night I left for college.

I was consumed with grief, which masqueraded as anger. In a long overdue moment of natural consequence, I banished our history, which I had rewritten into a tragic love story.

"When I agreed to surrendering our son, I had no help from you or your family. But the biggest deception of all was that the adoption was supposed to be better for *him*. He says that his adoptive parents love him, keep him safe, and treasure him as a chosen child. I believe him, but it wasn't US loving him, keeping him safe, treasuring him. You don't get to be happy now when all you do is leave." I was inconsolable.

There on I-70 East, the highway between Lawrence and Kansas City, feelings I had repressed finally emerged in full battle array. Joe had returned to his side of the car, but he insisted on holding my hand. He wasn't talking much to me, but I had his attention. I wanted him to *feel* the loss and grief as I did. I had found that level of empathy among other birthparents, but I wasn't feeling it from my son's birthfather. It was as though I was telling him a story in which he had no part, and I was beginning to surrender the deep belief that I could or should create an unlived life with the accidental father of my first child.

My fantasies of *what could have been* if Joe and I had married were washed up along the shore of my new reality. I saw all of it for what it was—a youthful misstep that created a lovely young man. There was no returning to the seventeen and eighteen year old teenagers we were in 1963. There was no alternate reality.

Joe offered little but quiet acquiesce to my words. He didn't attempt to justify anything that we hadn't already covered in my diatribe. I doubt that he'd had this deep level of conversation with anyone since I got on that train to Denver in 1965. He seemed unable to do or say anything to fix my pain.

What I was experiencing was loss and unspent grief with no time stamp, a self-sustaining virus of body and soul, able to mutate and emerge at any moment. It erupted this night after the reunion that I had been so proud to orchestrate, after the touching vision of father and son at the same dinner table, hugging, talking about sports, and discovering family history. That moment at the steakhouse was everything I thought I had wanted. Instead, I had stepped on a land mine of emotions. Finally, all was exploding.

I had opened a sealed box labeled, *ADOPTION FEELINGS*. I opened it with complete disregard for caution on behalf of finding my son and introducing him to his father. In the process, I had gained a child I could introduce to everyone in my life, but I worried that my son hadn't gained a devoted birthfather. Why was I surprised?

We arrived at Kansas City International Airport and sat at the curb for some time. Neither of us knew what to say or how to say it. It had been a long day, a difficult drive, and we were both exhausted. I was resigned to the fact that I had introduced father to son, and now I needed to go home and attend to my obvious healing.

When my son married a decade later, his birthfather came to the wedding. I was nervous to see Joe again, and I forewarned my husband and children that he would be in attendance. I walked our neighborhood in all weather for months before the wedding, thinking about how I would handle interacting with him. I bought a gorgeous Nolan Miller suit with tiny gold embroidery on the lapels. It was my color of blue and I looked trim and pretty. My hair was even behaving itself.

The wedding was at the Kansas City church where my son had graduated high school and attended mass—the same church where I had fervently prayed in 1963 when I lived with the doctor. The November day was lovely, and the color of my suit coordinated perfectly with the attendants and with the dress of my son's adoptive mother. My new daughter-in-law, whose mother died when she was a teenager, had invited me to help her choose her wedding dress, so I had a vested interest in this day on multiple levels. I had now become much more fully integrated into my son's life. I had been invited to showers, had hosted the engagement party, and had become a helpful mother-in-law-wedding-consultant as the day approached.

Although Joe would be attending the wedding, he would be arriving and departing the same day. As I waited for my son's brother to walk me down the aisle to our family pew, Joe came into the vestibule of the church. For a brief moment, something was and wasn't tangible—the *could have been* intersecting with *what was*. I was happy to see him, and he sat on the other end of the same row, next to my oldest daughter.

When the bride and groom met at the altar, I felt grateful to the powers that be for allowing me to be present at my son's wedding. I could easily have missed this day along with all the events in my son's life that had come and gone without me. Having his adoptive mother and his birthmother sitting one row apart for such an auspicious occasion seemed to suit our son just fine. He beamed as he posed in a photo with Joe and me. We were a good-looking trio, similar in noticeable ways, proud and courageous in ways that only I could fully know.

Joe came to the reception, but left after a brief stay. Maybe he was nervous, or maybe he really did have a plane to catch. I stayed up the night before the wedding because I had so many thoughts to sort out. I ended up writing a letter to Joe instead of sleeping, and I gave it to him as I walked him to his car.

When I handed him the letter, he said, "Is this a bill?"

To which I replied, "It should be."

We hugged each other, and he said something about *staying in touch*. He drove away to his real life, while I returned to our son's party.

Joe and I didn't stay in touch, and I never knew what he thought of my letter, but it was written as much for me as it was for him. Putting words on paper that night provided a way to end this chapter of my life, which was in need of finality and resolution:

Dear Joe:

I awoke this morning knowing I wanted to

share some thoughts and feelings with you. Certainly, it's the occasion—this day, that means so much more than we could have envisioned thirty years ago. Thirty years ago we were children ourselves, practicing adulthood, knowing passion, and searching outside ourselves for completion.

For the first time in all these years, which have passed in a moment, I realize how important it was for us to have known each other then, and what that means today. A part of me has always been sad that my first sexual experience, my first opportunity to be "in love," to truly give a part of myself to another person I loved, carried such a weighty consequence.

When I brought it from my head to my heart, I began to heal, to understand, to pull the ends of the circle together—to recreate myself. I was scattered all over the place, unknown even to myself, yet deliberately self-centered out of a sense of survival. Since finding our son, I have allowed that protective armor to fall away, piece-by-piece. Though the discovery was accompanied by another kind of pain, at least it was comprehensible. This wedding represents the culmination of all my self-reflection, my struggle to understand, to right the image of myself, and to clearly see what really happened between us, then and later.

The common thread is us. When we met, I held something precious within me that I intended to save, according to my Catholic Church and *Seventeen Magazine*, for marriage. But, life had other plans that included you. Not unwillingly, but certainly with a feeling of immortality and innocence, I changed my mind.

Even considering how short-lived our abandon was to be, how excruciating it became in reality, and the cost to us both, I've never regretted that choice. Now I can know why. The reason was before you today. That young man whom we created in 1963, for whatever physical and mystical motivation, is the result. Rather than see it as a collection of losses—of my virtue, whatever that means, and the opportunity to parent him, I see it as an enormous and valuable investment. The return is a dividend that begins today.

For one brief moment in time when I found our son, it may have been just when he needed us most, we were there for him. We were there for him today, too. It was good and right that we should share that moment, as we've shared so many before this. No, I don't regret what we've learned or how we've grieved in our own way and together. There is a lot of high energy and quicksilver magic about us. Perhaps the only way to transfer that combination into the world was to put it into our finest and only creation.

I'm proud that you are our son's father and that I am his mother. I am also happy to be your friend and to know that you were my first love.

     As Ever,
     Sharon

X
Green Ribbon
(Epilogue)
Olympia
2011

It's been more than thirty years since Lee Campbell opened the door to my soul on *The Phil Donahue Show*. It's been a few less since I met my surrendered son in a neighborhood park in Kansas City.

What happened to me and to other women is passé. Being single and having a baby has shed its stigma. Women have babies without having husbands every day. *Baby Daddy* is the cute name for the father who has absented himself or who has been declared extraneous.

Something has shifted that could not have been predicted in the 1960s. With a doctorate in psychology and a master's degree in social work, and almost two decades of university teaching, I have found my story valuable in a far different way than if it had only remained the stuff of family secrets.

My relationship with my beautiful, first child has been neither perfect nor easily interpreted. I am certain that we are both better off for what we know rather than what we might have imagined. The truth is out and he knows *why* and *how* the events happened as they did in 1964. I believe my decision to travel up the down staircase to find him—engaging in blatant rule breaking and truth bending—was wise. I couldn't remain silent while he was out there wondering why I had left him.

My son and I have talked from the beginning about *why* and he seems as satisfied with the answer as I am in telling it. There will always be the silent space between us, the boy-shaped hole in my heart and in my reality. We have figured out how to be *us* and he has graciously included me in his life, from those first college months to this very day as he celebrates his forty-seventh birthday. We had a long conversation in honor of this birthday, and he told me about my evolution in his mind from older sister, to aunt, to mother. His adoptive mother is much older than me, which means he may need more of me one day.

I met his parents for the first time at his college graduation. His adoptive mother tolerated me, his grandmother did not, and his father welcomed me, saying that I belonged exactly where I was standing, next to *our* son. My son's adoptive father was gracious and generous. I tried and failed to be his mother's friend.

Jim Gritter, the social worker who pioneered Open Adoption, writes:

> What the adoptive parents fear most is the birthmother's badness, when what they really fear is the birthmother's goodness . . . In adoption, grief is a moving target.

The first five years of our relationship did not involve his adoptive parents at all, so we had time to set our course and to become acquainted. We had time for him to meet the rest of his maternal and some of his paternal family, to take his sixteen-year-old sister for her driver's license test (twice), to attend family graduations, weddings, holidays, birthdays.

When he initially told his parents about my presence in his life, the timing was his choice and I honored that as I have his other choices since. I was the first to know when he thought that he was in love with the woman of his dreams. I held their engagement party at my house. His mother hosted the bridal shower, and I was invited. My family sat in the second row at his wedding, as did his birthfather, Joe. I often wonder what it must have been like for him to gain his independence and find an extra mother at the same time.

I tried to understand the depth of his adoptive mother's fears about me. I know it wore on him occasionally, but I assured him that I would step aside if he wanted me to. She was, in fact, his *mother*. He carved a place for me amidst her resistance and that of his beloved grandmother. My son honored all of us. I am never more proud of him than when he speaks his truth and steps into his place in our lives.

He introduces me as his *Birthmom,* and I'm sure he enjoys the ripple we create with our astonishing boldness as we claim our legitimacy. Of course, we're only eighteen years apart in age, and we could be taken for siblings. He teases me now, instructing me to stop looking so young because I make him look old.

In a perfect world, I would have been able to keep my child *and* raise him *and* go to school *and* have the life to which I was destined. I am often called upon to speak at professional conferences about issues of grief and loss. It's been a while since I've included this story among those I tell. I teach my students that the one commonality we share, maybe the only certainty among us, is our experience of loss. We are a grieving species. How we interpret it and how we see it as the lesson it is, allows us to grow beyond the pain. Adoption can be, as one woman told me, "A cement truck full of grief."

We do what we can to make things right. For some formerly-labeled, *unwed mothers*, what is right for them is to live without knowing their children and to harbor their secrets forever. Maybe these women believe that they are protecting their surrendered children. That is what we were told. Among the benefits I enjoy in the relationship my son and I are inventing, is that I have been included in his life. There is a normalcy now that has grown over time, though while I am grateful, I am also aware of what can never be reconstructed or recaptured.

I was present when my son's first child was born, becoming a grandmother for the first time at age fifty. My granddaughter, a stunning redhead, is sixteen, and she and her father are like opposing magnets. My role is to offer support and counsel when asked. The topic lately has been the struggle between a spirited teenage daughter and her protective father. She's the upgraded version of me at that age, but she is equipped with information and birth control. I also have another granddaughter who will be in high school. The youngest, my grandson, is the mirror image of his father. I know this from a little collection of photos given to me by my son's adoptive mother. There aren't many, but these photos span infancy through high school, and they are treasured, although they remind me of the years I missed.

Over time, my son has become part of the family fabric we weave, we tear, and we repair. Marriage and family-making isn't a clear path, but one wherein everything is connected. My son and his birthfather, Joe, live in bordering states. They don't have much contact, but they are similar in ways that are astonishing. I am disappointed that his birthfather hasn't worked toward a deeper relationship, and I believe it's a lost opportunity for them both, but I am not in charge of all the players on this stage.

Since resentment is defined as, *taking poison and wishing the other person would die,* I try to avoid it. If I were allowed one regret, it would be that I knew nothing of self-determination when I was eighteen years old in

1963. I was on intimate terms with fear. My deepest, disempowering fears were rooted in the belief that I needed to satisfy a moveable feast of rules, which pleased everyone but me—parents, church, society. It's a deep-seated system that must be unlearned without replacing it with anger.

In the search for my son and in our subsequent relationship, I have sensed the approval and the ethereal guidance of my first parents—my deceased mother and my birthfather, shot down over a German field in World War II. I have since discovered that my father, while serving in the military, wrote numerous letters to my mother, replete with love, yearning, and certainty that he would return to her and to me, their baby. I imagine that my mother could only miss him as she considered the *what-ifs* that attach themselves to life thereafter. The road back to my son has been illuminated by those letters, which are tied with a green ribbon for safekeeping.

A shared philosophy, born of many conversations between my son and me as we explored the complexities of *why,* has brought us to our revelatory conclusion— exactly the right parents raised him and he was *intended* to be *their* son, too. They gave him what they knew and he grew under their loving guidance. The brief loving liaison between a young and passionate couple in 1963, provided him the vehicle and delivery system that deposited him into this world.

Perhaps in our journey we have gained more than we have lost. There exists an infinite and unconventional capacity to love and to be loved. My son and I believe that if one mother is great, two are better, and this applies to fathers, siblings, grandparents, uncles, aunts, and family histories—having more people to love is a good thing.

Sharon Estill Taylor, PhD is an educator, speaker, and writer. She is a retired professor from Saint Martin's University in Olympia, WA, where she taught psychology, social work, was chair of women's studies, and director of first year experience. She has taught social work at Arizona State University and has served as the clinical coordinator of an adolescent addiction recovery unit in a Kansas City hospital. Dr. Taylor is a frequently invited presenter at professional conferences where she speaks about issues of grief and loss. A Spiegel TV documentary film, *A Love in the Time of War: The Last Flight of Lt. Estill,* depicts her search for and recovery of her father's WWII crash site in Germany. *Phantom Son: A Mother's Story of Surrender* is Dr. Taylor's first book. She resides in Scottsdale, AZ. To learn more about Dr. Taylor and her work, visit: www.sharonestilltaylor.com

Resources

Recommended Books:

Stow Away. They told me to forget. And I did. Now my memory has mutiny in mind by Dr. Lee Campbell

Cast Off: They called us dangerous women. So we organized and proved them right by Dr. Lee Campbell

The Spirit of Open Adoption by Jim Gritter, LMSW

Lifegivers by Jim Gritter, LMSW

Hospitious Adoption by Jim Gritter, LMSW

Taking Down the Wall by Christine Murphy

The Girls Who Went Away by Ann Fessler

Born with Teeth: A Memoir by Kate Mulgrew

Film Suggestions (via Secret Sons and Daughters: Adoptee Tales from the Sealed Record Era secretsonsanddaughters.org):

A Girl Like Her

Adopted For The Life of Me

Philomena

Organizations:

Concerned United Birthparents was founded in 1975 by Lee Campbell and other birthmothers who surrendered children to adoption. www.cubirthparents.org

American Adoption Congress created in 1978 as a support organization for adoption search and reform. www.americanadoptioncongress.org

Publications by Two Sylvias Press:

The Daily Poet:
Day-By-Day Prompts For Your Writing Practice
by Kelli Russell Agodon and Martha Silano (Print and eBook)

The Daily Poet Companion Journal (Print)

Fire On Her Tongue:
An Anthology of Contemporary Women's Poetry
edited by Kelli Russell Agodon and Annette Spaulding-Convy
(Print and eBook)

The Poet Tarot and Guidebook:
A Deck Of Creative Exploration (Print)

Phantom Son
by Sharon Estill Taylor (Print and eBook)

Community Chest
by Natalie Serber (Print)

What The Truth Tastes Like
by Martha Silano (Print and eBook)

landscape/heartbreak
by Michelle Peñaloza (Print and eBook)

Earth, Winner of the 2014 Two Sylvias Press Chapbook Prize
by Cecilia Woloch (Print and eBook)

The Cardiologist's Daughter
by Natasha Kochicheril Moni (Print and eBook)

She Returns to the Floating World
by Jeannine Hall Gailey (Print and eBook)

Hourglass Museum
by Kelli Russell Agodon (eBook)

Cloud Pharmacy
by Susan Rich (eBook)

Dear Alzheimer's: A Caregiver's Diary & Poems
by Esther Altshul Helfgott (eBook)

Listening to Mozart: Poems of Alzheimer's
by Esther Altshul Helfgott (eBook)

*Crab Creek Review 30ᵗʰ Anniversary Issue
featuring Northwest Poets*
edited by Kelli Russell Agodon and Annette Spaulding-Convy
(Print and eBook)

Please visit Two Sylvias Press (www.twosylviaspress.com) for information on purchasing our print books, eBooks, writing tools, and for submission guidelines for our annual chapbook prize. Two Sylvias Press also offers editing services and manuscript consultations.

Created with the belief
that great writing is good for the world.

Visit us online: www.twosylviaspress.com